# English for Nurses

D. Thomas, B.A.
*Thomas Danby College, Leeds*

*and*

J. Thomas, B.Sc.
*Pontefract and District High School for Girls*

EDWARD ARNOLD

First published 1969 by
Edward Arnold (Publishers) Ltd
41 Bedford Square, London, WC1B 3DP

ISBN: 0 7131 4155 7

Reprinted (with amendments) 1972
Reprinted 1974, 1976, 1977, 1978

RECYCLED
PAPER

Printed in Great Britain by
Unwin Brothers Limited
The Gresham Press Old Woking Surrey England

# Preface

Most young persons who embark on a nursing career will have completed a foundation course in English. What this book sets out to do is consolidate and revise the knowledge gained in such a course and, wherever possible, present information, assignments and guidance that the nurse will find useful in the hospital situation. The idea is to present English as a 'living' subject relevant to the nurse and to nursing.

A primary aim of the book is to improve verbal communication in a field where accurate communication is—to say the least—essential. A nurse must be able to understand instructions quickly and thoroughly, and execute them efficiently. It is also the book's intention to give the nurse an insight into the history of nursing and medicine, and to present a picture of today's scene, in the hope that this knowledge will help her to appreciate the position she holds within the service. In fact, the book is an attempt to help the nurse to come to terms with her job.

The approach the teacher adopts will depend on many factors—personal judgment, teaching methods, the type of student, and the time available. Even a course stretching over two years or more will not give the average student sufficient time to complete *all* the exercises. It is not the intention for the student to plough through the book from beginning to end. Instead, the teacher must carefully choose exercises to suit the students' needs and abilities, reserving the more difficult sections for the more advanced students. Much of the material can be presented more attractively if supplemented by suitable audio-visual material (see pp. 129–32) and visits to places of interest.

The book contains sufficient information and exercises to cover all 'O' Level syllabuses in English Language, or the equivalent first examination or leaving examination. For those students already in possession of such a qualification, the book offers the opportunity to stretch their abilities still further. They are encouraged to carry out project work, to participate in class assignments, to express themselves, and are prompted to think deeply into some of the many problems facing the profession today. All these go far to cater for the needs of most students in this field, whether they are preparing for an examination or, like a growing number of people, see better English as a passport to self-improvement.

*July, 1972*

D. Thomas
J. Thomas

# Acknowledgements

The authors wish to extend their thanks to those authors and publishers who kindly gave their permission to quote from the following publications:

*The History of Public Health*—Arthur Swinson, Wheaton Press, 1965.
*The Story of Health*—A. and G. Howat, Pergamon Press, 1967.
*The Book of Scientific Discovery*—Dr. D. M. Turner, Harrap, 1960.
*Vaccines*—Group Information Dept., Pfizer.
*Baillière's Pocket Book of Ward Information*—Marjorie Houghton (1965); *Baillière's Nurses' Dictionary*—revised by Barbara F. Cape (1964); *Aids to Bacteriology for Nurses*—Bocock and Armstrong (1962); *Aids to Anatomy and Physiology for Nurses*—Katherine F. Armstrong (1964). Baillière, Tindall and Cassell.
*Man against Disease*—Geoffrey Lapage, Abelard-Schuman, 1964.
*A Short History of Medicine*—F. N. L. Poynter and K. D. Keele, Mills & Boon, 1961.
*Science and the Doctor*—F. R. Elwell and J. M. Richardson, Bell, 1957.
*Great Lives*—Vol. 5 of the *Oxford Junior Encyclopaedia*, Oxford University Press, 1960.
Fowler's *Modern English Usage* (2nd edn., Gowers, 1965) Oxford University Press.
*Pears Cyclopaedia* (76th edn.)—Pelham Books.
*The National Health Service and You*—Gordon Thomas, with Dr. Ian D. Hudson, Panther (1965).
*The Story of Medicine*—Kenneth Walker, Hutchinson, 1954; Grey Arrow edition, 1959.
*Human Biology* (1960) and *Health, Personal and Communal* (1959)—John Gibson, Faber & Faber.
*Approach to Living*—Redifussion Television Ltd.
*Really, Nurse!*—Roger Brook, Souvenir Press (1960); Pan Books (1966).

Special thanks are also given to the editors of the *Nursing Mirror*, the *Nursing Times* and *The Yorkshire Post* for granting permission to quote from those publications, and to our colleague Albert Thornton, who did the illustrations.

# Contents

v

## PART V: SOME SPELLING AIDS                     *page*

## PART VI: PUNCTUATION

## PART VII: SOME USEFUL AUDIO-VISUAL MATERIAL

## PART VIII: LIST OF RECOMMENDED BOOKS

Part I
# HISTORY OF MEDICINE

# Milestones in Medical History

The doctors of ancient civilisations recognised many diseases, and had some useful methods of treating them. But until scientific methods were applied to the study of the body and its diseases, doctors could make only limited progress in overcoming the problems caused by the diseases afflicting mankind. People were virtually defenceless against such killers as the plague, [1] smallpox, yellow-fever, and cholera, as well as a great many lesser ailments.

Modern medicine is said to begin with Vesalius (1514–64), who laid the foundation for a scientific study of the human body. Another great advance was made when the English doctor William Harvey (1578–1657) investigated the circulation of the blood. Since then a series of great scientists and medical researchers have continued to add to our understanding of how the body [2a] works, as well as the differing natures of diseases.

One of the scientists was Edward Jenner (1749–1823), who developed the use of vaccination. He infected healthy people with cowpox, thus mobilising the natural defences of their bodies against the much more dangerous smallpox germ. Smallpox still survives in many developing countries, but it has been almost eliminated from Britain and other countries by vaccination and [2b] the isolation of people who may carry the disease.

It was the French scientist Louis Pasteur (1822–95) who established, by the most rigorous experiments, that the ancient doctrine of the 'spontaneous generation' of life was untrue. He made it clear that germs come from other germs, and discovered vaccines against anthrax and rabies. Building on the work of Pasteur, Lord Lister (1827–1912) developed the use of antisepsis, making it possible for the first time to conduct operations with the reduction [2c] of the grave danger that the patient would die of infection.

Another great advance in the battle against infectious disease was made by Paul Ehrlich (1854–1915) who studied the symptoms of lead poisoning in rabbits, and realised that if body cells had a way of selecting dyes, then dyes could be used to carry chemical messages to certain parts of the body. Eventually he discovered his 'magic bullet'—Salvarsan, which destroyed the spirochete of syphilis within the body. This was the beginning of great advances in chemotherapy. In 1932 the German chemist Gerhard Domagk began to experiment with the red dye prontosil and found that it would cure streptococcal infections. From this discovery came the wonderful series of sulphonamide drugs. No less inspired was the discovery that a certain mould exuded a substance which would kill germs. This led to the development of

penicillin and a great variety of other antibiotics which cope with many
[2d] infectious diseases.

Infectious disease is only one of several types of disease which plague mankind. Another major set of diseases are the result of faulty nutrition. In this
field one of the pioneers was Justus von Liebig (1803–73), who also did a great
deal for agriculture. Liebig divided foodstuffs into two main classes—those
which supply energy (sugars and fats) and those which build up new tissue
and repair wear-and-tear (proteins). But this was only the beginning. Later
scientists discovered that the body also needs small quantities of a number of
accessory food factors now called vitamins. Shortage of these essential food
factors produces diseases like scurvy (once common on sailing ships) and
rickets (which causes children to grow up with twisted bones and stunted
bodies). Today, people in countries like Britain eat a varied diet, and such
diseases are almost unknown; but vitamin deficiency is very common in
under-developed countries, as is the disease kwashiorkor, caused by lack of
[3] protein.

Mental disease is still common all over the world, though great strides have
been made in treating it in recent years, through drugs, shock treatment and
psychotherapy. Degenerative disease (e.g. cancer) is one type of disease which
is still not properly understood, and which often resists man's attempts at
[4] cure.

One of the most interesting of modern developments in medicine is the
establishment of 'spare-part surgery'. It is now possible to insert into the body
mechanical substitutes for certain parts of the body, such as valves of the
heart. It is also possible to replace organs, such as a kidney, with organs from
[5] another human being.

The work of public health departments in preventing disease, by improving
sanitary conditions and other means, has been just as important in lowering
the death rate and fostering good health as the more spectacular achievements
of the scientists in developing methods of combating disease once it has
[6] started.

[The above passage—taken from the Independent Television for Schools'
publication *Approach to Living* (Spring, 1968)—is reproduced by kind
permission of Rediffusion Television Ltd., the producers of the series.]

1   (i) Find synonyms, i.e. words of the same meaning, for the following
        words taken from the passage:

        afflicting (1), investigated (2a), eliminated, isolation (2b), spontaneous,
        developed (2c), selecting, exuded (2d), deficiency (3), fostering (6).

        Write sentences to illustrate the above words.

    (ii) In your own words explain what is meant by:

        (a) 'mobilising the natural defences of their bodies' (2b);
        (b) 'the ancient doctrine of the "spontaneous generation" of life' (2c);
        (c) 'accessory food factors' (3).

    (iii) Explain the difference between:

        (a) vaccination and inoculation; and
        (b) antisepsis and asepsis.

(iv) Give the meaning of the following terms used in the passage:

chemotherapy, streptococcal infections, antibiotics, proteins, vitamins, psychotherapy, degenerative diseases.

2 (i) Complete the following table by giving the passage a new title of your own choosing, finding a suitable heading for each section, and an appropriate sub-heading for each sub-section. *This will give you an idea of the structural plan of the passage.*

Title⋯⋯⋯⋯⋯⋯⋯⋯⋯⋯⋯⋯⋯⋯⋯⋯⋯⋯⋯⋯⋯⋯⋯⋯⋯⋯⋯⋯⋯⋯⋯⋯⋯⋯⋯⋯⋯⋯
Section 1⋯⋯⋯⋯⋯⋯⋯⋯⋯⋯⋯⋯⋯⋯⋯⋯⋯⋯⋯⋯⋯⋯⋯⋯⋯⋯⋯⋯⋯⋯⋯
   ,,   2⋯⋯⋯⋯⋯⋯⋯⋯⋯⋯⋯⋯⋯⋯⋯⋯⋯⋯⋯⋯⋯⋯⋯⋯⋯⋯⋯⋯⋯⋯⋯
        2a⋯⋯⋯⋯⋯⋯⋯⋯⋯⋯⋯⋯⋯⋯⋯⋯⋯⋯⋯⋯⋯⋯⋯⋯⋯⋯
        2b⋯⋯⋯⋯⋯⋯⋯⋯⋯⋯⋯⋯⋯⋯⋯⋯⋯⋯⋯⋯⋯⋯⋯⋯⋯⋯
        2c⋯⋯⋯⋯⋯⋯⋯⋯⋯⋯⋯⋯⋯⋯⋯⋯⋯⋯⋯⋯⋯⋯⋯⋯⋯⋯
        2d⋯⋯⋯⋯⋯⋯⋯⋯⋯⋯⋯⋯⋯⋯⋯⋯⋯⋯⋯⋯⋯⋯⋯⋯⋯⋯
   ,,   3⋯⋯⋯⋯⋯⋯⋯⋯⋯⋯⋯⋯⋯⋯⋯⋯⋯⋯⋯⋯⋯⋯⋯⋯⋯⋯⋯⋯⋯⋯⋯
   ,,   4⋯⋯⋯⋯⋯⋯⋯⋯⋯⋯⋯⋯⋯⋯⋯⋯⋯⋯⋯⋯⋯⋯⋯⋯⋯⋯⋯⋯⋯⋯⋯
   ,,   5⋯⋯⋯⋯⋯⋯⋯⋯⋯⋯⋯⋯⋯⋯⋯⋯⋯⋯⋯⋯⋯⋯⋯⋯⋯⋯⋯⋯⋯⋯⋯
   ,,   6⋯⋯⋯⋯⋯⋯⋯⋯⋯⋯⋯⋯⋯⋯⋯⋯⋯⋯⋯⋯⋯⋯⋯⋯⋯⋯⋯⋯⋯⋯⋯

(ii) Explain why the doctors of ancient civilisations made only limited progress in their fight against disease. (Make a list of other factors not mentioned in the passage.)

(iii) Construct a table listing all the scientists mentioned in Section 2, and state the contribution each made to the progress of medicine.

(iv) What are the two main methods used to eliminate highly contagious and dangerous diseases such as smallpox?

(v) Using not more than **sixty-five of your own words**, make a summary of Section 3.

(vi) What three methods mentioned in the passage have been used with much success to treat mental illnesses?

(vii) State what is meant by the term 'spare-part surgery', and explain the importance of this field of surgery.

(viii) Describe the main aims of the public health authorities.

(ix) From the information given in the passage, attempt to make a simple classification of diseases.

**RESEARCH.   In each case state the source of your information**

3 (i) Write *short notes* on the following diseases mentioned in the passage. Describe their symptoms, causes, and recommended treatment.

smallpox, yellow-fever, cholera, anthrax, rabies, scurvy, rickets, kwashiorkor, cancer.

If you wish, you may set out your answer in the form of a table.

(ii) Write *brief* biographies of the following doctors and scientists mentioned in the passage.

Vesalius (1514–64), William Harvey (1578–1657), Edward Jenner (1749–1823), Louis Pasteur (1822–95), Lord Lister (1827–1912), Paul Ehrlich (1854–1915), Gerhard Domagk (1895–1964), Justus von Liebig (1803–1873).

(iii) Write *brief notes* on the development, application and effectiveness of the following drugs mentioned in the passage:

Salvarsan, sulphonamides, penicillin.

(iv) What do you consider to be the *three* most important medical discoveries mentioned in the passage? Qualify your answer.

(v) Write an essay on any *one* of the following. Add a *bibliography*, i.e. add a list of the books you consulted when writing your essay. Give the title of each book, the edition, the author, publisher, and the year of publication.

(a) *Our Diet* (traditional eating habits; effects of poor diet; a balanced diet; people's varying needs).
(b) *Main Sources of Food* (cereals, dairy produce, meat and fish, vegetables, fruit).
(c) *Modern Food Technology* (hygiene, processing, additives, etc.).
(d) *Nutrients in Food* (carbohydrates, fats, proteins, vitamins, mineral substances).
(e) *The Effects of Cooking Our Food.*
(f) *Sources of Water Supply* (well, stream, reservoir, treatment, plant, etc.).
(g) *Water: Friend or Foe?* (Importance to body, agriculture, etc.; water-borne diseases, flooding, drought, etc.)

# Madhouses to Mental Hospitals

One of the greatest revolutions in our thinking during the last hundred years has been in our attitude to mental illness. Today, mental cases form a large percentage of hospital admissions, but we realise that disorders and diseases of the mind can be treated just like physical injuries or influenza, or tonsillitis, and in the majority of instances a complete cure is effected. In the eighteenth century, people whose minds were afflicted were known as lunatics and were confined, often in isolation, in workhouses, prisons and hospitals. Village idiots were often chained to posts; and even George III was put into a strait-jacket. The first legislation to attempt any regulation of madhouses was an Act of 1774. It applied only to private madhouses and did not cover private hospitals, but it did institute a system of inspection. Nothing was done by way of providing buildings until the Act of 1808 gave powers to the Justices of the Peace in every county in England to build proper houses for the reception of such lunatics 'as were chargeable on their respective parishes'. Some of the asylums built under this Act, such as at Chester and Lancaster, are still being used. The main achievement of the Act was to effect the removal [1] of insane people from the workhouses and prisons.

In 1815 (the year of Waterloo) a select committee was appointed to consider provisions for the better regulation of madhouses, as the buildings available were now inadequate. When the report of this committee came out it showed that, apart from buildings, the care of the insane was disgraceful. In Bethlem hospital, for example, Edward Wakefield, a land agent who had taken upon himself the duty of visiting madhouses to try to help their occupants, found these conditions:

> One of the side rooms contained about ten patients, each chained by one arm or leg to the wall; the chain allowed them merely to stand up by the bench or form fixed to the wall, or to sit down on it. The nakedness of each patient was covered by a blanket gown only. . . .

Godfrey Higgins, who had taken over the York asylum, told the committee how he found some rooms tucked behind the kitchens. At first the keepers said the keys had been lost, but eventually produced them. Higgins walked inside and found that:

> There were four cells about 8 feet square, in a very horrid and filthy situation; the straw appeared to be almost saturated with urine and

5

excrement; there was some bedding laid upon the straw . . . the air holes, of
which there was only one in each cell, were partly filled in. I asked the
keeper if these cells were inhabited by patients, and was told that they were
at night. I then desired him to take me upstairs and show me the place of
the women who came out of these rooms that morning. . . . He showed me
into a room which I caused him to measure, and the size of which was 12
feet by 7 feet 10 inches. In it were thirteen women whom he told me had all
[2]    come out of those cells that morning.

Through the nineteenth century the accommodation and general care of the
insane gradually improved, though a select committee sitting in 1827 found
that things were just as bad as in 1815. The Lunacy Act of 1845, which set up a
Board of Commissioners with Lord Shaftesbury as chairman, was the first
major piece of legislation. The commissioners sent two of their own number,
one legal and one medical, to visit every hospital once a year, and private
asylums twice a year. The Act also made regulations for doctors who were
called upon to certify people as insane, giving some protection to the patient.
In 1877 a Committee of Inquiry found that the number of insane people in
[3] need of care was 64,916 and that the figure was rising each year.
    In the eighteen-seventies and eighteen-eighties there was a great deal of
discussion about lunacy, but the legal aspects were now over-shadowing all
thoughts of care, let alone treatment. In what circumstances should a person
be certified insane? How should one protect an elderly person, for example,
from greedy relatives wanting to get him out of the way? On the other hand,
how should the law be framed so that it was not so difficult to have a person
certified, that, by the time the formalities had been completed, it was too late
for any treatment? The upshot of all this debate and argument was the Lunacy
Act of 1890, which offered a compromise that satisfied almost no one. Part of
the trouble, no doubt, was that it was still impossible to distinguish between
temporary disorders capable of treatment, and congenital disorders brought
[4] about by some physical defect in the brain.
    This position continued until 1904 when a Royal Commission was set up
'To consider the existing methods of dealing with idiots and epileptics, and
with imbeciles, feeble-minded or defective persons not certified under the
lunacy laws' and to recommend changes in the law 'due regard being made to
the expense involved in any such proposals'. The Commission deliberated for
four years and no legislation was passed until 1913, when the Mental Deficiency
Act was brought in. This split mentally affected people into four categories:
idiots; imbeciles; the feeble minded; and moral defectives. There is no need
to consider at length the machinery set up for registering and caring for these
cases, though in passing we should note that there was still no hint that mental
illness should be treated as *an illness* as opposed to a permanent state. It was
not in fact until 1926 that a Royal Commission was appointed to inquire
(amongst other things) 'the extent to which provision is or should be made for
the treatment without certification of persons suffering from mental disorder:
and to make recommendations'. What the Commission found was that the
arrangements for caring for the insane still smacked of the Victorian Poor
Law rather than enlightened twentieth-century medicine. To put things right
they recommended that 'the treatment of mental disorder must be made to
approximate as nearly to the treatment of physical ailments as is consistent with

the special safeguards which are indispensable when the liberty of the subject is infringed; certification should be the last resort and not a preliminary to treatment . . .'. Also it argued that the procedure for certification should be simplified and should be the same for all whether they were private or rate-aided cases, and that it should be 'dissociated from the Poor Law'. In 1930 the Mental Treatment Act was passed and led to an immediate improvement in the situation. At last the modern development of psychiatry was brought into play, child guidance clinics were set up, and arrangements were made for the training of psychiatric social workers. All the services dealing with the care and prevention of mental illness were integrated under the National Health [5] Act of 1946.

[The above passage, taken from Arthur Swinson's *The History of Public Health* (Wheaton Press, Exeter, 1965) is reproduced by kind permission of the author and publishers, Pergamon Press Ltd., Oxford.]

1  (i) Find suitable synonyms to replace the following words used in the passage:

    afflicted, confined, reception (1), saturated (2), indispensable, infringed (5).

  (ii) Write sentences to illustrate the meaning of the following words:

    isolation (1), formalities, compromise, congenital (4), defective, dissociated, integrated (5).

 (iii) Find out the origin of the following words:

    tonsillitis, lunatics, congenital.

 (iv) **In your own words**, differentiate between each of the following types of mentally afflicted person:

    idiots, imbeciles, the feeble minded, moral defectives (5).

2  (i) Give the passage a new title, and each section a suitable heading:

    Title.............................................................................................................
    Section  1...................................................................................................
       ,,  2......................................................................................................
       ,,  3......................................................................................................
       ,,  4......................................................................................................
       ,,  5......................................................................................................

  (ii) In one sentence describe how the twentieth-century attitude to mental illness differs from, say, the eighteenth-century attitude.

 (iii) What provision in the 1845 Lunacy Act was inserted to safeguard the freedom of the individual?

 (iv) In your own words, re-write the words that Godfrey Higgins delivered to the 1815 select committee on the regulation of madhouses.

(v) From the information given in the passage, complete as much of the following table as you can:

(vi) What does the author mean when he writes that 'in the 1870s and 1880s . . . the legal aspects were over-shadowing all thoughts of care, let alone treatment'?

| Act | Provisions | Results |
|---|---|---|
| 1774 Act | | |
| 1808 Act | | |
| Lunacy Act, 1845 | | |
| Mental Deficiency Act, 1913 | | |
| Mental Treatment Act, 1930 | | |
| National Health Act, 1946 | | |

(vii) Explain why the 1890 Lunacy Act 'offered a compromise that satisfied no one'.

(viii) Why, in the words of the author, did the Royal Commission of 1926 come to the conclusion that 'certification should be the last resort and not a preliminary to treatment'?

**RESEARCH.** In each case acknowledge the source of your information

3  (i) Using the following plan as a basis, write an essay entitled *The Changing View of Insanity*.

(a) The Theory of Devil Possession.
(b) The Attitude of the Church.
(c) The Fifteenth Century and the Witch Theory.
(d) The Unreformed Asylums.
(e) The Reformers: Dr. Philippe Pinel, William Tuke, John Conolly, Lord Shaftesbury (7th), Dorothea Lynde Dix.

(ii) Write an essay entitled *The Modern Treatment of Neurosis and Psychosis*. The following is suggested as a plan:

(a) Difference between Psychosis and Neurosis.
(b) Convulsive (or Shock) Therapy.
(c) Pre-frontal Leucotomy.
(d) Psychology, psychotherapy, group therapy, occupational therapy.
(e) The Psychiatric Social Worker.

(iii) Write a short essay on any ONE of the following:

(a) Faith Healing.
(b) The Christian Scientists.
(c) 'Placebos'.
(d) The Development of Psychology—drawing attention to the work of such people as Alfred Adler (1870–1937), Carl Gustav Jung (1875–1961), Sigmund Freud (1856–1939).

## Discussion topics

(I) John Barrymore (1882–1942), a famous American actor, once stated: 'America is a country where you buy a lifetime's supply of aspirin for one dollar, and use it up in two weeks.' What did Barrymore mean by this, and to what extent do you think it now applies to life in this country?

(II) Consider and discuss this case: A mother of two young children needs an emergency blood transfusion if she is to survive an accident received when being driven home by her husband. He is unhurt. Being a Jehovah's Witness she refuses the necessary medical aid, and so dies. Her husband comments later to the press: 'I feel proud that my wife was able to make this supreme sacrifice for her principles.'

Do you think that in such circumstances a qualified medical practitioner should be given the authority to administer essential medical aid even against the wishes of the individual concerned?

(III) To what extent do you think that anti-social behaviour stems from some kind of mental disorder? Before you begin, decide among yourselves what the term 'anti-social behaviour' means.

(IV) Although the progress in treating the mentally afflicted has in many ways been colossal—particularly the advances made in medical knowledge—there is still room for much improvement. Bearing in mind that the number of mental cases increases annually, do you not think it time that the Government instituted an emergency programme to build sufficient mental hospitals, equip them, and recruit the necessary staff? Or do you think there are other more pressing priorities than the care of the mentally ill? If so, what are they?

# The Fight against Pain

Man's search for an efficient anaesthetic has a very long history. Many believe that the *nepenthe* mentioned by Homer was nothing more than what we now know as opium, most probably used by Greek doctors as a soporific. Later, the Arabian physicians used both opium and hyoscyamus. The narcotic properties of mandrake (or mandragora) were known even before these times; and from Elizabethan times frequent mention is made of the drug. Alcohol, too, has at various times found a place as an anaesthetic, but however much successful in stupifying a patient before an operation, it has its obvious [1] disadvantages.

The first real piece of progress was made in 1799 when Sir Humphry Davy (inventor of the miner's safety lamp) inhaled nitrous oxide and noted its results. Although he realised the pain-killing properties of the gas (later to be known as 'laughing gas') and suggested its use for surgical operations, the medical profession did not take advantage of the discovery until many years later. In fact, it was not until 1844 that a young American dentist by the name of Horace Wells (of Hartford, Connecticut) used the gas for painless tooth extraction. Wells had used 'laughing gas' successfully on many occasions, but when he came to the crucial demonstration before a distinguished medical audience at the Massachusetts General Hospital, Boston, the patient groaned and the audience, considering the operation a failure, refused to be convinced of the value of nitrous oxide as an anaesthetic. This occurred in January, [2] 1845.

Another step forward in inhalation anaesthesia also occurred in the 1840s. On this occasion, sulphuric ether was the substance that attracted medical attention. Although William E. Clarke, of Rochester, U.S.A., had used it successfully in January, 1842, for the painless extraction of a young lady's tooth, he did not follow up his work. This was left to W. T. G. Morton, a former pupil of Horace Wells and a witness to his teacher's 'failure' at Boston in January, 1845. In September, 1846, he used ether for a tooth extraction, and on 16 October he demonstrated its use at the Massachusetts General Infirmary, where he used it for the successful operation for the removal of a [3] neck tumour.

The first operation to be carried out under a general anaesthetic in England was performed by Robert Liston at the University College Hospital, London, where on 21 December, 1846, he amputated a patient's leg. Like Morton, Liston used ether. In January of the following year, Sir James Young Simpson of Edinburgh used ether in obstetrics. This caused a storm of indignant protest from many theologians, who considered the use of anaesthetics in a normal delivery as being against God's will, but it failed to stop Simpson. In

10

November, 1847, he was using chloroform both in obstetrics and for general
[4] surgical operations.

The rapid acceptance of nitrous oxide, ether and chloroform was accompanied by the adoption of new surgical skills and techniques. Instead of speed, a primary requisite before anaesthesia, the surgeon concentrated on neatness and thoroughness. Together with antisepsis, pioneered by Joseph Lister, it also prepared the way for those daring and elaborate operations that were to
[5] take place before the turn of the century.

With anaesthetics came a new profession, that of the anaesthetist. One might say that the first professional anaesthetist was John Snow (1813–58), notable for his chloroform inhaler. An immediate successor to Snow, and a person who improved upon Snow's method of administering chloroform, was Joseph Thomas Clover (1825–82), whose inhaler consisted of an airtight bag containing a mixture of chloroform and air prepared in advance. It was safer than Snow's method, but it suffered from the disadvantage of being rather too clumsy for general use. The next refinement of note came from Sir Francis Edward Shipway, who devised an apparatus that allowed the anaesthetist to use varying concentrations of chloroform and ether, and to mix these with oxygen. But even this must be considered a rather clumsy affair when com-
[6] pared with the equipment at the disposal of the modern anaesthetist.

The concept of a local anaesthetic—something that would kill pain in a localised area without the patient losing consciousness—is also something that is not new. Even in early times, many South American tribes were aware of the pain-killing properties of the coca plant. If at any time an incision had to be made, then coca leaves were chewed, and the saliva allowed to run over the
[7a] area to be cut.

During the mid-nineteenth century German chemists managed to extract from the coca plant a substance known as cocaine. As a pain-killer this was first used on the surface of the skin, but later two other methods were used: in one, the cocaine was injected under the skin; in the other, injected into the nerve trunks. The surgeon accredited with the first successful use of cocaine was Carl Koller (1857–1944), who used it with much success in eye and nose surgery. In recent years, the use of cocaine has been superseded by several synthesised derivatives of cocaine, such as novacaine and stovaine, which combine the advantages of cocaine with a greater degree of
[7b] safety.

The last quarter of the nineteenth century saw much pioneer work in other forms of anaesthesia: cocaine, for instance, was injected into the spinal cord to produce analgesia in the legs; rectal anaesthesia was attempted and, although initially unsuccessful, progress was made in the early part of this century; and, finally, endotracheal anaesthesia, valuable for operations to the mouth and jaw, was introduced. A recent innovation is the use of intravenous injections of curare which, used in conjunction with an anaesthetic, produces perfect
[8] muscle relaxation.

Today, a person having an operation is generally nervous because he has to look forward to a short period of relative discomfort. Gone are the days when a visit to the surgeon—even for what today we consider a minor operation— was anticipated with dread. And with reason, for the patient had little to look forward to but excruciating pain and a pretty good chance of not returning
[9] home.

1  (i) Replace each of the following words by an appropriate word or short phrase:

   demonstrated (3), indignant (4), elaborate (5), devised (6), excruciating (9).

  (ii) Write sentences to illustrate the meaning of any **five** of the following words:

   soporific (1), crucial (2), requisite (5), refinement, disposal (6), concept, incision (7a), anticipated (9).

 (iii) Differentiate between each of the following:

   inhalation anaesthesia (3), rectal anaesthesia (8), endotracheal anaesthesia (8).

 (iv) What does the term *analgesia* mean?

  (v) Write a short paragraph on each of the following:

   opium, hyoscyamus, mandragora, cocaine, curare.

2  (i) Give the passage a new title of your own choosing, under which write down appropriate headings for the sections, and sub-headings for the sub-sections. This will give you the structural plan of the passage.

  (ii) Construct a clear, well-labelled chart illustrating the advances made in the field of anaesthetics since Greek times.

 (iii) What are the 'obvious disadvantages' of alcohol as an anaesthetic?

 (iv) Give two examples taken from the passage to illustrate the reluctance of the medical profession to accept change readily; and then give another example to show how it forced change in spite of the reluctance on the part of others.

  (v) Why do you think that dentists rather than doctors used anaesthetics first?

 (vi) The acceptance of anaesthetics in the mid-nineteenth century led to two major developments in surgical practice. What were they?

 (vii) What advantage did Clover's chloroform inhaler have over Snow's? What was its own major disadvantage?

(viii) Summarise Section 7 in not more than **eighty of your own words.**

 (ix) Under a suitable heading, make a list of some of the ways that surgery today differs from the surgery in the early nineteenth century.

**RESEARCH. In each case, acknowledge the source of your information**

3  (i) What are the two main purposes of an anaesthetic?

  (ii) Explain the difference between a *light* anaesthetic and a *deep* anaesthetic.

(iii) There are two types of *general* anaesthetic: inhalation and intravenous. Give three examples of each.

(iv) Make a list of the main disadvantages of chloroform.

(v) Why should ether *not* be used when performing a cautery?

(vi) When was aspirin introduced? What is its scientific name?

(vii) In what year was phenacetin discovered? For what was it originally used?

(viii) Name at least three local anaesthetics in general use today.

(ix) What is the common name for Hyoscyamus Niger?

(x) Find a Shakespearean quotation referring to Mandrake (or mandragora).

# Antisepsis and Asepsis: The Contribution of Lord Lister

Joseph Lister (1827–1912) was the son of a wine merchant who was a spare-time scientist interested in working with microscopes. He entered University College Hospital in London as a student and was lucky enough to attend the first operation under ether in Britain. He spent seven years as a surgeon in
[1] Edinburgh, and then became professor of surgery in Glasgow in 1860.

The surgical wards at Glasgow Royal Infirmary had been built over the burial place of the victims of a cholera epidemic in the city only eleven years before. This fact was blamed for the very high death rate of those who had been operated on. Victims of compound fractures, those where the bone breaks through the skin, were also likely to die if the limb were not amputated soon after the accident. In his studies of inflammation, pus formation and gangrene, Lister thought that some outside agent was the cause rather than just the bad air of an industrial area. He then learnt of Pasteur's work and realised that the outside agent was germs, introduced through accidental or operation
[2a] wounds.

At this time a surgeon would put on a dirty frock coat for the operation, which was probably stiff with the blood of previous victims. The operating theatre would not be clean, nor would the instruments. Even the surgeon's hands might be dirty. These were the conditions that led to so much infection and subsequent death. Operations were more frequent after the discovery of
[2b] anaesthetics, but they were dreaded just as much.

Lister first put his new ideas to the test in his treatment of compound fractures. He dressed the wounds with carbolic acid before immobilising the limb. The acid might burn the patient's skin, but at least it killed the germs. Later he used weaker solutions of acid, and used them after operations. But he went further than mere treatment of the wound. He insisted on cleanliness of operating theatre, instruments, surgeons and nurses. He made sure that hands were washed in a weak carbolic acid solution. At one time he had a spray of the acid throughout the operation. He wanted to prevent germs from getting into the wound rather than to kill them once they were there. So it was that
[3] Lister with his 'asepsis' made modern surgery possible.

His ideas were accepted throughout Britain except in London. And so it was in London itself that he took the professorship of surgery at King's

College when it was offered to him. Gradually he overcame his critics by his
[4] great success in preventing infection.

Lister devised many surgical instruments in use today. He also introduced
the use of catgut (made from sheep's intestines) in sewing up wounds, treating
it with carbolic acid. One of his favourite remarks was: 'There is only one rule
of practice: put yourself in the patient's place.' This he did, and deserved the
tributes that Pasteur and many others paid him. He was the first person to
be made a peer for his services to medicine, and was one of the original
[5] members of the Order of Merit.

At the very end of the nineteenth century Lister received the Freedom of
the City of Edinburgh. In his speech he said: 'I regard all worldly distinctions
as nothing in comparison with the hope that I may have been the means of
[6] reducing the sum total of human misery.'

[The above passage, taken from A. and G. Howat's *The Story of Health*
(Pergamon Press, 1967) is reproduced with the kind permission of the authors
and publishers.]

1 (i) In your own words, explain the difference between *antisepsis* and
  *asepsis*.

 (ii) Find out the etymology (i.e. the origin) of the following words:

  microscope (1), epidemic (2a), antisepsis, asepsis (3), intestine (5).

 (iii) Write definitions of the following:

  ether, compound fracture, gangrene, catgut, carbolic acid.

 (iv) Use the following words in sentences to show you can use them
  correctly:

  amputated, agent (2a), subsequent (2b), immobilising (3), devised,
  tributes (5), distinctions, comparison (6).

 (v) Write brief notes on each of the following types of gangrene:

  moist, dry, diabetic, gas, senile.

2 (i) Find the structural plan of the passage by giving each section a suitable
  heading and each sub-section an appropriate sub-heading.

 (ii) Construct a table (or diagram) pinpointing the main landmarks in
  Joseph Lister's life.

 (iii) Why did many people believe that the siting of Glasgow Royal
  Infirmary was a major cause of the high death rate among patients who
  had been operated on? Explain why this belief was erroneous.

 (iv) What factors made Lister realise that gangrene was caused by outside
  agents, viz, germs?

 (v) In not more than sixty of your own words describe the conditions of
  surgical operations before Lister's time.

 (vi) Make a list of the antiseptic and aseptic precautions Lister took to
  make operations safer.

(vii) What other contributions—other than the introduction of antiseptic and aseptic techniques—did Lister make to surgery?

(viii) Comment on Lister's dictum: 'There is only one rule of practice: put yourself in the patient's place.'

## RESEARCH.   In each case acknowledge the source of your information

(i) Name the surgeon who performed the operation referred to in Section [1], i.e. the first operation under ether in Britain.

(ii) Write a short history of either Glasgow Royal Infirmary
                    or King's College Hospital, London.

(iii) Distribute the following essay titles among the class members so that each subject is covered. On completion, each essay might be read out to the class and the author submitted to questions based on the essay.

(a) The Life and Work of Louis Pasteur.
(b) The Private Life of Joseph Lister.
(c) Lister's Contribution to Medicine.
(d) Pasteur's Contribution to Science.
(e) Surgery before the Three A's: Anaesthetics, Antiseptics, Asepsis.
(f) Modern Antiseptics.
(g) Asepsis Today.
(h) 'Whereas nineteenth-century medicine owed much to the chemist, twentieth-century medicine is greatly indebted to the physicist.'
(i) How far do you consider it true that the introduction of anaesthetics, together with the principles of antisepsis and asepsis, heralded a 'Golden Age of Surgery'?
(j) Throughout the nineteenth century, Science—particularly medical science—'fought a prolonged but successful battle against religious prejudice'. How far do you consider this statement valid?

# Our Growing Defences against Disease

Perhaps the most direct help from science in preventing sickness lies in the means it gives for destroying the organisms of disease before they begin their harmful attacks on man. The pasteurisation of milk, the sterilisation of water in public baths, and the treatment of sewage by which disease-bacteria are destroyed are methods which help towards the maintenance of general health. Those living in temperate lands can now congratulate themselves that hygienic methods have almost eradicated cholera, typhoid fever, small-pox and typhus. Those in warmer climates, however, are in constant danger from a number of diseases, the most widespread of which is malaria. Effective control of malaria can be brought about by destroying the mosquito at the larval stage. At one time this was done by the laborious process of treating the marshy lands with paraffin or oil, which reduced the surface tension of the water to such an extent that the mosquito larvae lost their hold on the under surface of the water and perished through lack of air. The more effective method now used consists of using the powerful insecticide D.D.T. dissolved in a suitable oil and sprayed on the land by hand or, still better, from aircraft. Another powerful insecticide, *Gammexane*, is also used to attack the mosquito in the
[1] adult as well as in the larval stage.

So far we have cited a few instances of successful prevention of infection. When, however, the micro-organisms have entered the human body recourse is made to a drug which will destroy the organism and yet be harmless to the tissue. A notable instance of such a direct-acting drug is Salvarsan, or 606, produced in 1909 for the treatment of syphilis. The long and very painstaking investigation which finally led to the discovery of Salvarsan and its success in relieving a great disease encouraged further search for chemical substances with specific therapeutic action. For a long time no compounds were found which were effective against common bacterial infections, and it was not until 1935 that pathologists in Germany announced that a red dye, *prontosil*, was
[2a] effective against a number of streptoccocal diseases. [2a] Soon afterwards, news came from the Pasteur Institute of Paris that only a part of the compound prontosil was active against bacteria, and that a simpler compound, *sulphanil-amide*, was the real agent. Immediately, systematic trials were set on foot in London, and laboratory researches, together with the resources of manu-facturing chemists, gave a series of drugs often known as *sulphonamides*, the
[2b] best known being M & B 693.

The sulphonamide drugs have been found to have a large margin of safety

17

and to be effective against a wide range of streptococcal infections, such as tonsillitis, pneumonia, puerperal fever, undulant fever and septicaemia. The mortality among mothers suffering from puerperal sepsis had already fallen to a low figure owing to the adoption of more rational and hygienic treatment. But the mortality became still lower after the use of the sulphonamide [2c] compounds.

Valuable though the sulphonamide drugs proved themselves to be, it was found that great care was necessary in their use, since toxic symptoms occasionally followed. In other words, these drugs not only attacked the disease-producing bacteria, but might attack the body cells of the human being harbouring those bacteria as well. Medical men therefore kept a weather eye open for more selective and perhaps more effective agents. Their search was not in vain, and within recent years a new class of substances called anti- [2d] biotics has been developed.

Antibiotics differ from other bacterial agents in being obtained from moulds or certain micro-organisms, which produce them in the normal course of their existence. Work is now proceeding on the synthesis of antibiotics in the laboratory. The action of an antibiotic is such that a susceptible micro-organism is unable to continue the chemical activities it needs for life. It has been found that antibiotics exist which attack in this way a wide variety of micro-organisms and yet have virtually no ill-effects on the functioning of the human body. Probably the best known of these is penicillin, which is effective against the organisms responsible for pneumonia and other serious diseases. Other widely used antibiotics include *streptomycin* and *aureomycin*, both of [3] which are active against certain bacteria which resist penicillin.

The discovery of penicillin was one for which physicians had been waiting since the days of Lord Lister. Although much had been learned since that time, Sir Alexander Fleming's studies of septic wounds during the First World War had shown that antiseptics then in use were often toxic to the body tissues as well as the invading bacteria. Now he had found an antiseptic that was innocuous to the body cells. As the name of the mould was *Penicillium notatum* he proposed to call the filtrate, from the broth in which the mould had been cultivated, penicillin, and this is the origin of that now familiar [4a] word.

The story now shifts to Oxford in 1939, where Sir Howard Florey and others were searching for antibacterial substances produced by micro-organisms. Florey succeeded in obtaining a brown powder far more bacteri-cidal than the sulphonamides, and able to inhibit the growth of Staphylococci in a dilution of 1 in 500,000. Curiously enough, when the isolation of penicillin in the pure form of its sodium salt had been accomplished it was realised that this brown powder contained 1 per cent. of penicillin and 99 per cent. impurities. Nevertheless early clinical studies in Oxford with the small amounts of penicillin then available were enough to show that an antibacterial substance of tremendous potency was now within reach. The problem, how- [4b] ever, was to find means for producing it in large enough amounts.

While methods for large-scale production were being perfected, meticulous research was continued in laboratories on both sides of the Atlantic. Investigations into the chemical nature of penicillin showed that there were four or more penicillins which have different degrees of effectiveness while in the living body. Close observations have resulted in methods by which the most therapeutically active penicillin, the so-called G compound, can be produced and preserved unchanged. For this purpose the technique for quick freezing and drying *in vacuo* (the method used for the preparation of human blood serum and plasma during the 1939–45 war) has provided yet one more instance of the close relationship between large-scale engineering techniques and [4c] fundamental research.

No antibiotics have been found that will attack true viruses without also attacking the body cells of the person harbouring the virus. The reason for this is that true viruses live in much more intimate association with their host than do bacteria, and consequently a chemical which disrupts the life processes of the virus is likely to disrupt those of the host cell as well. There are, however, large viruses intermediate in kind between bacteria and true viruses in that they are relatively independent of the host, and some of these have proved susceptible to antibiotics. Examples are the psittacosis virus (psitta-[5a] cosis affects parrots) and the virus-like organism that causes typhus fever.

Another limitation of antibiotics is that certain pathogenic bacteria have proved capable of adapting themselves to their new environment by developing strains which are resistant to antibiotics. The more these antibiotics are used, the more will resistant strains develop. Consequently, medical men do not prescribe these 'wonder drugs' without due caution. Nevertheless, anti-biotics remain a highly significant addition to our armoury of bactericidal [5b] chemicals. [*slightly abridged*]

[The above passage, taken from Dr. D. M. Turner's *The Book of Scientific Discovery* (Harrap, 1960), is reproduced by kind permission of the author and the publishers.]

1  (i)  Find out the meaning and origin of the following five words:

   pasteurisation, insecticide (1), puerperal, septicaemia (2c), toxic (4a).

(ii)  Complete the following table by inserting each of the following words into the relevant column, and then filling in the remaining blanks with the appropriate parts of speech derived from them:

   selective (2), inhibit, isolation, potency (4b), intimate, disrupt (5a).

|      | Nouns          | Verbs        | Adjectives |
|------|----------------|--------------|------------|
| e.g. | isolation (4b) | (to) isolate | isolated   |
|      |                |              |            |
|      |                |              |            |
|      |                |              |            |

(iii)  Compose dictionary-type entries for any **ten** of the following:

   malaria, cholera, smallpox, puerperal fever, undulant fever, septi-caemia, pathogenic bacteria, streptococcal diseases, sulphonamide drugs, penicillin, streptomycin, aureomycin.

(iv) Find suitable synonyms for any **five** of the following words that are used in the passage; use the remaining five in sentences to illustrate their meaning:

preventing (1), recourse (2a), rational (2c), harbouring (2d), susceptible, functioning (3), innocuous (4a), inhibit, accomplished (4b), meticulous (4c).

(v) Differentiate between:

(a) typhoid fever and typhus; and
(b) blood plasma and blood serum.

(vi) Study the spelling of the following words in preparation for a spelling test:

maintenance, hygienic, mosquito, laborious, paraffin, dissolved, therapeutic, streptococcal, symptom, pneumonia, independent, penicillin, aureomycin, septicaemia, puerperal.

2 (i) Complete the following table by giving the passage a new title, finding suitable headings for the sections and appropriate sub-headings for the sub-sections. This will give you the *structural plan* of the passage.

Title..................................................................................................................

Section 1..........................................................................................................

„      2..........................................................................................................

         (a)......................................................................................................

         (b)......................................................................................................

         (c)......................................................................................................

         (d)......................................................................................................

„      3..........................................................................................................

„      4..........................................................................................................

         (a)......................................................................................................

         (b)......................................................................................................

         (c)......................................................................................................

„      5..........................................................................................................

         (a)......................................................................................................

         (b)......................................................................................................

(ii) Under a suitable heading, make a list of some of the methods that have been adopted to *prevent* pathogenic bacteria entering the body.

 (iii) Using your own words, write a short paragraph on 'Controlling Malaria'.

 (iv) Any drug that is successful against bacterial diseases must possess two primary qualities. What are they?

 (v) What effect did the discovery of Salvarsan have on medical research?

 (vi) Make a list of (a) the main advantages and (b) the main disadvantages of the sulphonamide drugs.

 (vii) Explain how antibiotics differ from the 'other bacterial agents'.

 (viii) In simple terms, explain how penicillin works.

 (ix) Write a brief, note-form history of the discovery of penicillin.

 (x) What facts have come to light from research into the chemical nature of penicillin?

 (xi) Explain why antibiotics are generally ineffective against viruses.

 (xii) What are the two major disadvantages of antibiotics?

**RESEARCH. In each case, acknowledge the source of your information**

3  (i) Write brief biographical notes on the following, then choose any **one** for a more thorough examination, writing a detailed biographical essay covering his life, times, and work.

> Louis Pasteur        Selman Abraham Waksman
> Sir Alexander Fleming   Max Theiler
> Sir Howard Florey     Gerhard Domagk
> Ernst Boris Chain     Sir Ronald Ross

 (ii) Write an essay on any **one** of the following:

   (a) The Development of the Microscope
   (b) Recent Advances in Antibiotics.
   (c) The Fight Against Malaria (or Yellow Fever).
   (d) Man's Defences against Sleeping Sickness (or Undulant Fever or Endemic Syphilis).

 (iii) Write an account of an immunisation campaign carried out in your area, say, in the last 5–10 years.

## CLASS ASSIGNMENT

Using the following table as a guide, construct a wallchart entitled *Drugs that Changed the World*. Find drawings and photographs relevant to the main theme and add them to the chart. On completion of the chart, each student will be expected to extract from it the necessary information for the completion of the following table:

| Drug | Date discovered | Names associated with the discovery | Additional information |
|------|-----------------|-------------------------------------|------------------------|
| Morphine | | | |
| Quinine | | | |
| Codeine | | | |
| Cocaine | | | |
| Phenol | | | |
| Phenobarbitone | | | |
| Procaine | | | |
| Anti-Histamine | | | |
| Insulin | | | |
| Pentothal | | | |
| Sulphonamide | | | |
| D.D.T. | | | |
| Penicillin | | | |
| LSD–25 | | | |
| Streptomycin | | | |
| Aureomycin | | | |
| Cortisone Acetate | | | |
| Terramycin | | | |

# A History of Bacteriology

The history of bacteriology is short, but progress has been very rapid since the importance of bacteria as a cause of infectious diseases has been recognised. Exact bacteriological diagnosis and to a large extent diagnosis of virus-disease is now possible. Epidemics can now be controlled, and preventive medicine can do much to limit disease; and some outbreaks, like diphtheria epidemics, have been practically eliminated. The advance in modern surgery has come about only since, as E. G. D. Murray says, 'It has been lifted out of [1] the despond of laudable pus into the security of asepsis.'

For centuries, all races used the products of bacterial growth and fermentation without realising the implications of the changes or the processes involved. In fact, the relationship between fermentation and infectious disease was not suspected until two centuries after bacteria were first seen in 1676 by Antonius van Leeuwenhoek, using primitive microscopes of his own design and making.

In 1546 Fracastoro wrote a book on contagion and was the first to record that infection is composed of minute insensible particles and proceeds from them. He noted that the infection was the same for 'he who received as for he who had given' the infection. This was a great advance, recognising as it did the transmission of disease. Nevertheless, although contagion was generally recognised in some diseases, as in the plague and in syphilis, in others it was still missed.

In 1776 Spallanzani first cultivated bacteria in sterilised media, with and without air. He failed, however, to realise the importance of this and either [2] was unaware of Fracastoro's work or failed to relate it to his own.

While this work was being carried on by the scientists, the cause of infectious disease was being investigated empirically by the clinicians of the day. In 1767 Hunter, investigating the causative organisms of syphilis, experimentally infected himself. Unfortunately, he induced in himself a mixed infection of gonorrhoea and syphilis and his results were, because of this, confused. In 1796 Jenner introduced vaccination, making use of the practical belief that those who had cowpox were immune or partially immune to small- [3] pox.

It was not until 1847 that Semmelweis used the principle of ordinary social cleanliness to prevent sepsis. Dirt on instruments and skin acts as a binding agent for organisms, so the removal of extraneous dirt and grease did much to cut down sepsis by the removal of many of the pathogenic organisms, and was [4] a great step towards aseptic techniques.

The improvement in the microscope led to special diseases being associated with certain organisms of characteristic morphology. In 1850 Davaine saw

23

what he called minute 'infusoria' in the blood of sheep dead from anthrax, and
he was able to transmit the disease by inoculation of greatly diluted blood.
Subsequent work by Pasteur and Koch proved to be the starting point of
[5] bacteriology.

The techniques of modern bacteriology have developed greatly since the
science was begun by pure chemists, headed by Pasteur, whose interest
began with industrial fermentation problems. He demonstrated that alcohol
fermentation was brought about by specific bacterial enzymes, and gave a
logical explanation for a process which had been carried on for hundreds of
years. Pasteur's studies were widespread, involving the ripening and preserv-
[6] ing of wine, diseases of silkworms, and putrefaction.

Lister followed Pasteur's work on fermentation and carried out experiments
to test the deduction that if fermentation of sugar and starch was due to
bacterial action, sepsis and putrefaction of proteins were due to a similar
cause. He therefore attempted to prevent bacterial infection of operation
wounds and injuries and many forms of sepsis which resulted in suppuration,
hospital gangrene and septicaemia. He used carbolic, or phenol, to destroy
germs and prevent them gaining access to wounds, and published the successful results of his work in *The Lancet* in 1867, though it was a long time before
many of his sceptical colleagues accepted his teaching. By applying carbolic
putty to cases of compound fracture, he was able to save limbs which would
previously have been amputated because of the risk of a fatal result from
gangrene or septicaemia. He made it possible to operate safely within the
abdominal cavity and on joints and bones, developments which later, with
further advances in asepsis, antisepsis and anaesthetics, made every part of
[7] the body accessible to surgery.

While Pasteur was working in France and Lister in England, Koch in
Germany was developing bacteriological techniques which form the basis of
modern diagnostic bacteriology. Today it is relatively simple to identify an
unknown organism. The tests which are likely to be of use under given conditions have now been laid down (the routine in chemical analysis to discover
an organism might be likened to police work to discover a wrongdoer), but in
1870 Koch had no such rules to help him and new disciplines had to be worked
out. Koch isolated the bacillus of anthrax, and this was the first pathogenic
organism to be isolated in culture free from other organisms. He devised
liquid and solid culture media which included both serum and blood agar and
noted that the organism grew in clusters, called colonies, which eventually
became visible to the naked eye. He saw that these colonies were characteristic
and had defined conditions of growth. After this start, the causative organisms
of numerous other infectious diseases were isolated and their conditions of
[8] growth noted in the same way.

In 1881 Klebs and Loeffler isolated the diphtheria bacillus and later
workers grew tetanus organisms. The discovery of these organisms necessi-
tated a reassessment of the preformed theories of bacterial infection. It was
discovered that filtrates of growing cultures of these organisms (that is to say,
material in which the organisms had been growing but from which they had
been removed by means of filtration) were still able to cause death from
diphtheria. This led to the discovery of toxins, or powerful tissue-poisons,
often enzymes or ferments, which are produced by some organisms during
growth and secreted into the surrounding tissues to be carried through the

body in the blood stream. Organisms like the bacilli causing diphtheria and tetanus were found to be capable of growing in one part of the body and producing poisons which could be transmitted widely by the tissue fluids, [9] blood or nerves.

In 1890 von Behring showed that diphtheria could be prevented and cured by the administration of serum from a horse recovered from diphtheria. This was the discovery of antitoxins. In 1891 Ehrlich standardised diphtheria toxin so [10] that its potency could be assessed and the antitoxin measured against it.

In 1883 Metchnikoff, studying inflammation, called the polymorphonuclear white cells present in pus 'phagocytes' and he put forward the theory that these cells were protective in that they destroyed and engulfed the infecting [11] bacteria.

Less is known about the viruses than about bacteria. As has already been stated they are too small to be seen by the ordinary microscope although they can now be seen with the electron microscope. They will not grow on artificial media but require living cells inside which they multiply, that is to say they are intracellular parasites and their metabolism is closely bound up with the metabolism of the host cell. For these reasons the classical methods of study used in bacteriology are inapplicable and new ones have been, and are being, [12] devised.

[The above passage, taken from Bocock and Armstrong's *Aids to Bacteriology for Nurses* (1962), is reproduced by the kind permission of the publishers, Baillière, Tindall & Cassell.]

1   (i)  Find suitable synonyms for the following five words:

>     extraneous  (4),  diluted,  morphology  (5),  demonstrated  (6), defined (8).

(ii)  Use each of the following words in sentences to show that you can use them correctly:

>     eliminated (1), implications, contagion, transmission (2), empirically, induced (3), putrefaction, accessible (7), isolated (8), potency (10).

(iii)  Differentiate between (a) 'gangrene' and 'septicaemia';
                             (b) 'bacteria' and 'viruses'.

(iv)  **In your own words**, write brief, accurate definitions of the following terms:

| | |
|---|---|
| fermentation (2) | pathogenic organisms (4) |
| bacterial enzymes (6) | suppuration (7) |
| blood agar (8) | liquid and solid culture media (8) |
| toxin (9) | antitoxin (10) |
| phagocytes (11) | electron microscope (12) |
| intracellular parasites (12) | metabolism (12). |

(v)  Explain what is meant by the following:

(a) 'It (i.e. modern surgery) has been lifted out of the despond of laudable pus into the security of asepsis' (1).
(b) '. . . the cause of infectious disease was being investigated empirically by the clinicians of the day' (3).

(c) 'It was not until 1847 that Semmelweis used the principle of ordinary social cleanliness to prevent sepsis' (3).

2  (i) Supply the passage with a new, more exciting, title. Having done that, give each section a heading. This will give the structural plan around which the authors built the article.

Title:..................................................................................................
Section 1..............................................................................................
    „    2..............................................................................................
    „    3..............................................................................................
    „    4..............................................................................................
    „    5..............................................................................................
    „    6..............................................................................................
    „    7..............................................................................................
    „    8..............................................................................................
    „    9..............................................................................................
    „   10..............................................................................................
    „   11..............................................................................................
    „   12..............................................................................................

(ii) Make a list of some of the beneficial results of the progress made in bacteriology.

(iii) Write a note-form summary of Section 3.

(iv) Why were the results of Hunter's investigations into the causes of infectious diseases said to be 'confused'?

(v) Jenner's work on the smallpox vaccine was based on a common belief. What was this belief?

(vi) In your own words, explain why Semmelweis's practice of 'social cleanliness' was a great step towards aseptic techniques.

(vii) What was so important about the discovery made by Davaine in 1850?

(viii) In one sentence, state Pasteur's contribution to bacteriology.

(ix) (a) Under a suitable heading, explain Lister's method of achieving asepsis; and
(b) also under an appropriate heading, make a list of the immediate results of Lister's methods of antisepsis.

(x) The advances made in surgery during the latter half of the nineteenth century were the results of progress made in the '3 A's'. What were these?

(xi) Why is it relatively easy today to recognise different bacteria?

(xii) What was Koch's main contribution to bacteriology?

(xiii) Why did the results of Kleb's and Loeffler's work on diphtheria necessitate 'a reassessment of the preformed theories of bacterial infection'?

(xiv) What are 'toxins'? How did bacteriologists become aware of them?

(xv) Using one sentence for each, explain the contribution made to bacteriology by (a) Behring in 1890, and (b) Ehrlich in 1891.

(xvi) In your own words, explain Metchnikoff's 'phagocyte' theory.

(xvii) Why are the methods used to study bacteria inapplicable to the study of viruses?

## RESEARCH.   In each case acknowledge the source of your information

3   (i) Name five common diseases caused by bacteria.

(ii) Find out the scientific names for the bacteria that cause the following diseases:

(a) anthrax            (b) tetanus
(c) bacillary dysentery   (d) tuberculosis
(e) diphtheria         (f) pneumonia

(iii) Find out the number of people who died from diphtheria in England and Wales in:

(a) 1875    (b) 1900    (c) 1925
(d) 1945    (e) 1955    (f) 1970

# The Fight against Virus Infection

The fact that many diseases do not attack the same person more than once was first recorded by Thucydides. The great historian observed that the plague which killed more than a quarter of the Greek population during the Peloponnesian Wars conferred immunity upon those who survived it. Twenty-two centuries later, in 1792, the British physician John Hunter visualised a possible relationship between the blood and the body's defences against infection—foreshadowing by 100 years the observations of Buchner and Pfeiffer that led Ehrlich to propound the theories on which the modern con-
[1] cept of immunology is based.

Without belabouring the details of immunological concepts, let us merely state that when many complex chemical substances, foreign to the body ('antigens'), gain entrance to the body tissues the body produces specific substances ('antibodies') in an effort to rid itself of them. Antibodies are generally specific in action and are usually defined by the way they act: 'Lysin' dissolves foreign substances, 'agglutinin' causes them to clump (particularly in the case of bacteria), and 'precipitin' causes blood-soluble substances (like bacterial poisons) to be neutralised by precipitation. Thus, in a healthy person, the fate of foreign substances that gain entrance to the body is sealed by the
[2] antibodies produced in response to them.

At least 4,000 years ago an astute Chinese physician observed that the powdered crusts of a smallpox infection, when blown into the nostrils of a healthy person, appeared to reduce the severity of a later infection and—many times—prevented the disease. In the England of George I, Lady Montagu, wife of the British ambassador in Turkey, introduced an eagerly welcomed and widely practised 'inoculation' method of controlling this blinding, scarring and killing pox. She taught physicians to draw a thread soaked in the fluid from a smallpox pustule, through a superficial incision in the arm. But the real conquest of the disease can be attributed to Edward Jenner, who, on 14 May, 1796, 'vaccinated' an eight-year-old boy with pus from the hand of a Gloucestershire dairymaid infected with cowpox. Eight weeks later Jenner inoculated the lad with smallpox—and no disease appeared.

Both diseases, smallpox and cowpox, are caused by viruses—micro-organisms too small to be seen with an ordinary microscope. And the method Jenner used, or variations of it, eventually proved to be medicine's most powerful weapon against virus disease.

Jenner used the virus of a mild disease to provoke immunity to a major one.

He was very lucky; smallpox happens to be the only known disease in which
[3] this particular technique is useful.

In trying to find a cure for rabies, Louis Pasteur was forced to use the
virulently infective materials of the disease itself, there being no closely
related illness. His solution was to modify the agent that caused it by infecting
rabbits with it. The spinal cords of the dead rabbits were then hung up to dry;
in the course of about fifteen d₵  ₎ these cords became progressively less
capable of causing the disease when ground up and injected into dogs. By
running the injections in reverse—giving the oldest cord preparation first,
and then moving progressively to the fresh cord preparation—Pasteur
in 1884 succeeded in producing a vaccine which gave immunity against
[4] rabies.

Though he was thoroughly familiar with bacteria, Pasteur never saw the
organism that causes rabies. The existence of an infectious agent smaller than
the bacteria was not suggested until 1892, just three years before Pasteur's
death and four years after his active life in science had been permanently
interrupted by ill health.

In 1898, the German bacteriologist F. A. J. Loeffler confirmed suspicions
that infectious material from the hoof and mouth disease of cattle can be
passed through a filter which stops all bacteria, and still remain infectious.
Walter Reed and the Yellow Fever Commission demonstrated in 1900 that
the same is true of yellow fever, and in 1903 the French physician R. Rem-
linger discovered that rabies was also caused by an agent that would pass
[5a] through a bacterial filter.

That poliomyelitis is a virus disease was established by Simon Flexner in
1910 after Landsteiner demonstrated that the disease can be given to monkeys
by injection of human material. What was now urgently needed, however, was
a method of growing viruses in larger quantities, in order to provide sufficient
[5b] material for the preparation of vaccines.

This was a difficult problem, for the viruses cannot be cultivated on artificial
media in the way that bacteria can. The first laboratory breakthrough came in
1913, when a team of three scientists—Steinhard, Israeli and Lambert—
utilised the then new technique of tissue culture to grow viruses. Tissue
culture is a technique which permits the growing of isolated animal tissues in
test tubes and flasks. For virus culture, where the organism will grow nowhere
but inside a living cell, isolated growing tissues are an obvious culture
[5c] medium.

A less difficult technique, however, was discovered in 1931, when vaccinia
virus was successfully cultivated for the first time in chick embryos. The rapidly
propagating cells of the chick inside the egg provide a convenient living culture
chamber, containing everything the virus needs to prosper, free from the
elaborate maintenance and sterility requirements of the tissue culture method.
[5d] In short, it is cleaner, quicker and cheaper.

The most important organisms which have been adapted to chick embryo
culture thus far are: yellow fever (1938); rabies (1939); Newcastle disease
of poultry (1944); mumps (1945); and canine distemper (1949). [*slightly*
[5e] *abridged*]

[The above passage has been taken from *Vaccines*, a paper prepared and distributed by the Group Information Department of Pfizer Ltd., Sandwich,
Kent.]

1  (i) Find suitable synonyms for each of the following words used in the passage:

   conferred, visualised, propound, concept (1), astute, severity, attributed (3), permits (5c).

  (ii) Write sentences to illustrate the use of the following words as they are used in the passage:

   belabouring, specific (2), variations, provoke, technique (3), modify (4), confirmed (5a), utilised (5c), propagating (5d).

 (iii) Explain what is meant by:

      (a) 'complex chemical substances' (2);
      (b) 'superficial incision' (3);
      (c) 'virulently infective materials' (4).

  (iv) **In your own words**, explain the difference between:

      (a) an 'antigen' and an 'antibody'; and
      (b) 'tissue culture' and 'chick embryo culture'.
      (c) macule, papule, vesicle, pustule.

2  (i) Section 1 acts as an introduction to the article. Give it a suitable heading, and then re-write the section in your own words.

  (ii) Supply Section 2 with an appropriate heading.

 (iii) To what extent is it true to say that 'antibodies are generally specific in action'? Quote three examples to illustrate your answer.

  (iv) Re-write Section 5 in **not more than 100 of your own words.**

   (v) James Phipps, the eight-year-old boy whom Jenner vaccinated in 1796, was lucky in more ways than one. Explain this.

  (vi) Supply Section 4 with a suitable heading; then, **in your own words**, explain the method Pasteur used to create immunity to rabies.

 (vii) Explain why Pasteur did not see the organism that causes rabies.

(viii) Find a relevant heading for Section 5, and sub-headings for sub-sections 5a, b, c, d, and e.

  (ix) Under a suitable heading, make a list of the advantages of cultivating vaccines in chick embryos.

### RESEARCH.  In each case acknowledge the source of your information

3  (i) Name five common diseases caused by viruses.

  (ii) What are 'lymphocytes', and where in the body are they produced?

 (iii) Why is it difficult to produce vaccines against the common cold?

### CLASS ASSIGNMENT

*Suggested approach:* Split the class into nine pairs or groups, each one to be responsible for writing a 500–700 word article and making a wallchart (or series of charts) on **ONE** of the following:

(i) Types of Bacteria.     (ii) Bactericides.
(iii) The Spread of Bacterial Infection.
(iv) Protection against Bacterial Diseases.
(v) Types of Immunity.     (vi) Virus Infections.
(vii) The Nature of Viruses.     (viii) How Vaccines are Developed.
(ix) The Spread of Virus Diseases.

[The completed essays and wallcharts—under the general title of, say, 'Man Against Disease'—would make a very impressive display.]

# The Work of the Surgeon (I)

With aseptic methods, developed as a result of a great deal of careful research, came the use of new materials for making ligatures and entirely new methods of preventing loss of blood while operations were being performed. The discovery of blood groups and of blood transfusions contributed greatly to the revolution in surgery that then occurred and this, together with equally remarkable discoveries of new and better anaesthetics and killers of pain, eventually gave us the largely bloodless and completely aseptic surgical
[1] marvels of our time.

Some of these marvels are so recent that you may actually have seen surgeons doing them on the television screen. To discuss all the patient research that has led to them would occupy much more space than we have. The materials nowadays used for stitching up wounds, for example, are the outcome of experiments that began in the time of Galen (A.D. 130–200), when surgeons used hemp and silk and catgut. Trials continued through the use of various materials taken from animals, such as strips of skin, the tendons of horses, whale and kangaroo, pieces of blood vessels and nerves and even horse hair. Lister himself tested many materials, soaking them in carbolic acid before they were used. Apart from the problem of the material used, experiments were also done to test the effects of tying knots in these materials. Some were discarded because they lost their strength when knots were tied in them, or because some strands tended to break. Others were rejected because they would not withstand the actions of the fluids of the body, or because they irritated the body tissues—a failing especially of wire threads or other materials which created sharp angles or end in sharp points. At the same time it was remembered that it was an advantage to use, for some purposes, materials which would eventually be absorbed by the body, provided, of course, that they remained intact long enough to perform their function
[2] properly.

There was, too, the problem of the actual knots that surgeons used. These have to be free from any tendency to slip and the surgeon has to be expert in tying them. This is especially important when, as often happens, they are in a small space at the bottom of a deep dissection he has made. Various knots have been invented and also various kinds of needles, curved and straight, with which the stitches are inserted. The modern surgeon's stitchcraft is, in
[3] fact, one of his most valuable accomplishments.

Finally we must mention one broad aspect of modern surgery, one of its most dramatic and beneficent aspects. In 1873 there was born at Lyons, in France, a man named Alexis Carrel, who in 1900 took his medical degree at Lyons University. He became a surgeon and was especially interested in surgical experiments, particularly in trying to work out methods of joining together the ends of arteries and veins that had been ruptured or severed. In 1902 he published in France a method of doing this. Soon after, Carrel showed how blood vessels could be kept for long periods in cold storage and could then be transplanted into the body to take the place of damaged blood vessels in it. In 1904 he went to the University of Chicago to pursue this line of work and later to the Rockefeller Institute for Medical Research in New York. His idea now was to remove, not merely blood vessels, but whole organs, from the body and to keep them alive outside it. For this purpose he needed a machine which would pump blood through the organs thus removed and it had to be, of course, a machine that would also keep the blood free from bacterial [4a] infection.

The problem of how to construct such a machine was too difficult for Carrel. He needed the help of someone who knew all about machines and also how to make them. As Calder relates, he succeeded in finding someone who could do this difficult job. This was the American airman Charles Lindbergh, who was already famous for being the first person to fly the Atlantic Ocean alone. Lindbergh eventually produced ( : machine called the Lindbergh Pump, which is described in Carrel's book, *The Culture of Organs*.

Carrel claimed that whole organs could be removed from the body and put into the Lindbergh Pump in which they could, he claimed, be treated more [4b] effectively than while the organs were still inside the body.

But this was not all that Carrel did. In collaboration with the French surgeon, Theodore Tuffier, who was a pioneer in chest surgery, he did a number of successful operations on the valves that direct the course of the [4c] blood inside the heart.

Carrel's work on heart operations will live with that of another Nobel Prize winner, Werner Theodor Forssmann. Forssmann was the first man to show that it is possible to introduce a tube into a vein in the arm and to pass it along this into the heart. But he differs from other pioneers in one important respect. He did this remarkable experiment, not on an animal, but on himself. In 1929, when he was twenty-five years old, he was working at the August Victoria Home at Eberswalde, near Berlin. One day, when he was alone, he introduced a tube into the vein on the front of his elbow and pushed it gently up the vein until he thought it had reached his heart. Having walked along to the X-Ray Department, he was there able to verify, by means of an X-ray photograph, that the tube had in fact arrived in his heart. A month after this a colleague drew attention to the work of three other German investigators. They had previously introduced tubes into the heart in a similar way, but had done this [5] on patients under their care.

Experiments like this one of Forssmann's, and many others which developed Carrel's work, have led to the astonishing operations that are nowadays safely performed. Often these are on vital organs such as the heart, blood vessels, lungs, nerves, brain, and organs in the abdomen. They have also led to the machines which are used to temporarily replace vital organs such as the kidneys; or which, while operations on the heart are being performed, drain off the blood passing through the heart, keep it supplied with oxygen, and then [6] return it to the body.

There are, too, such feats as the one accomplished not so long ago in America, when a healthy 7 lb. baby was removed from the womb of its

mother by the operation called Caesarean section. This operation has, of
course, been a commonplace of surgery for many years; but this mother upon
whom the American surgeons operated, was also suffering from paralysis of
one leg, which was due to the kind of swelling called an *aneurysm* on the large
artery that supplies the leg. This paralysis the surgeons cured by replacing the
swollen part of the artery with a plastic tube which by-passed the swelling.
Finally, as the unfortunate mother also suffered from a leaking heart valve, they
gave her a necessary rest from the operating table and then successfully
[7] repaired the leaking valve.

Operations of this marvellous and elaborate kind are, in fact, increasing in
their daring and complexity. Dr. C. Walton Lillehei, for instance, the expert
in operations on the heart at the College of Cardiac Surgery in Los Angeles, is
quoted as having recently said that surgery is nowadays definitely in sight of
being able, in suitable cases, to transplant a heart from one body to another,
or to put inside the chest a completely mechanical heart instead of the normal
one. This replacement of the heart by a mechanical device has in fact been
successfully done in the dog. And the heart beat, when it goes wrong, can
nowadays be successfully controlled and made to beat normally by a transis-
torised 'pace-maker'. This is inserted into a pocket in the abdomen and is
connected with the heart by wires which transmit the electric current from the
small batteries in it. These batteries do not run down for several years and
with this device the unfortunate sufferers from this derangement of the heart
[8] are enabled to live and work quite normally.

We should never forget how these and all other marvels of modern surgery
have been made possible. They were developed by the devoted and highly
skilled work and knowledge of teams of experts working with equally highly
skilled surgeons. We owe them, too, to the chemists who have produced, by
long and laborious experiment, the marvellously pleasant modern anaesthetics which do away with the pain and shock that surgical operations used
to cause. Truly, we must be grateful, especially when we remember that these
astonishing advances have all been made in the last sixty years or so. [*slightly*
[9] *abridged*]

[The above passage, taken from Geoffrey Lapage's *Man Against Disease*
(Abelard–Schuman, 1964) is reproduced by the kind permission of the author
and publisher.]

1  (i) Complete the following table by inserting suitable synonyms and
    antonyms for the words in the first column:

|                  | Synonyms | Antonyms |
| --- | --- | --- |
| construct (4b)   |          |          |
| verify (5)       |          |          |
| vital (6)        |          |          |
| elaborate (8)    |          |          |
| complexity (8)   |          |          |
| devoted (9)      |          |          |

   (ii) Write sentences to illustrate the meaning of any **five** of the following words:

      contributed (1), discarded (2), beneficent, pursue, collaboration (4), accomplished (7).

  (iii) Explain the difference between (a) 'ruptured' and 'severed' (4a);

                    and (b) 'ligatures' and 'sutures'.

  (iv) Write a brief definition of each of the following:

      ligatures (1), hemp (2), carbolic acid (2), Caesarean section (7), aneurysm (7).

2  (i) The passage refers to many advances that have made surgery safer and the surgeon's work easier. Under a suitable heading, make a list of **all** the advances mentioned.

  (ii) Using not more than **eighty** of your own words, write a summary of Section 2. Place your summary under an appropriate heading.

  (iii) What prompts the author to state that 'the surgeon's stitchcraft is one of his most valuable accomplishments'?

  (iv) From the information given in the passage, write a note-form biography of Alexis Carrel.

  (v) What was the purpose served by the Lindbergh Pump, and what qualities did it possess?

  (vi) What was the major contribution Forssmann made to surgery, and what factors helped to make this even more remarkable? Choose up to five adjectives that you think best describe Forssmann.

  (vii) Re-write the information given in Section 7 as you think it would have appeared in (a) the *Daily Mirror*, and (b) the *Guardian*. Supply your articles with suitable headlines.

 (viii) Make a list of examples to support the author's statement that 'operations . . . are increasing in their daring and complexity'.

  (ix) Although the surgeons have tended to take the limelight for the remarkable operations that have been performed over the last hundred years or so, they owe their success to the work of people in other fields. Name some of these related fields.

  (x) Construct an outline plan of the passage by giving each section a relevant heading and each sub-section a suitable sub-heading. Place these under a title of your own choosing.

**RESEARCH.**  **In each case acknowledge the source of your information**

3  (i) Give the name of the person who discovered the existence of blood groups.

  (ii) What differentiates one blood group from another? How many blood groups are there, and what are they?

(iii) Write brief biographical notes on (a) Werner Theodor Forssmann; (b) Theodore Tuffier; (c) Charles Lindbergh; (d) Alfred Nobel.

(iv) In what year, where, and by whom, were the following operations first successfully carried out?

    (a) removal of a brain tumour;
    (b) removal of a cancerous lung;
    (c) operation on a heart valve;
    (d) kidney transplant;
    (e) tumour removed from spinal cord;
    (f) heart transplant.

**CLASS ASSIGNMENT.** For this, the class can be split up into pairs or small groups, each to be responsible for completing an essay on one of the following subjects. Where possible, illustrate the work with suitable diagrams, sketches, photographs, cuttings, etc.

(a) *Pioneer Work in Plastic Surgery.*
(b) *Plastic Surgery Today.*
(c) *Blood Groupings: An Explanation.*
(d) *The Blood Transfusion Service.*
(e) *Spare-part Surgery: A Progress Report.*
(f) *Heart Transplants: A History.*
(g) *Transplants: The Moral Issues.*
(h) *The Problems of Tissue Rejection.*
(i) *Preventive Medicine: Is the State doing enough?* (Legislation against smoking, drinking, 'smog', noise, traffic, etc.)

# The Work of the Surgeon (II)

The spectacular progress which surgery has made in the last ten years can, however, only partly be attributed to our success in minimising hazards. Many of the astonishing operations performed today have as their essential basis the knowledge and skill and experience which has been patiently accumulated for the last two generations. During that time many surgical 'specialities' have become firmly established: the surgery of the brain and the central nervous system, of the thorax and lungs, of the heart and blood vessels, of the stomach and intestines; plastic and orthopaedic surgery. Men and women of great ability have spent their whole lives in study and work in each of these fields, and with this unprecedented concentration on clearly defined problems the answers were at times found theoretically before the technical means were available to demonstrate them, and often long before the most daring surgeon thought it safe to apply them in practice. Advances in every field of medical knowledge have now combined with phenomenal progress in
[1] technology to make many of the older surgeons' dreams come true.

The pioneer of modern brain surgery was an Englishman, Sir Victor Horsley, who worked at the National Hospital for Nervous Diseases, in Queen Square, London. He was successfully removing tumours on the brain in the 1890s, and the war in which he met his death (in Mesopotamia in 1916) was the great opportunity for his most brilliant pupil, Harvey Cushing, the American surgeon, to go far beyond his master and become the most influ-
[2] ential specialist in this field.

Modern plastic surgery also had its origins in the First World War, although some of its practical techniques are ancient and were originally devised in India. There, one of the most common punishments for malefactors was the cutting off of the nose and the Hindu surgeons worked out a method of repairing this disfigurement by using a graft from the forehead. Until the seventeenth century, Venice was the great meeting place of the East and West, so it was no accident that it was a Venetian surgeon, Gaspare Tagliacozzi (1546–99), who, at the end of the sixteenth century (notable for endemic syphilis, which also destroys the nose), introduced this eastern secret to European surgeons. We do not know how much it was practised—there were certainly few great exponents who have left records of their work. One who did was a London surgeon named Carpue who performed a number of successful
[3a] operations on soldiers wounded in the Napoleonic Wars.

It was the war of 1914–18 which produced its greatest modern practitioner, Sir Harold Gillies, who worked for years on patients so disfigured by wounds that they were kept in a special hospital. The Second World War, with its numbers of airmen burned in crashed aircraft and its civilians burned and

37

wounded in incendiary raids on towns and cities, allowed Gillies' pupil, Sir Archibald MacIndoe, to show how far this skill could be developed. They both died in the same year (1960), but they have left their pupils to carry on the [3b] work in every part of the world.

Much knowledge of a fundamental nature has arisen out of this work. The surgeon has often dreamed of the possibility of transplanting organs—new kidneys, new hearts for old—but in fact it has been found that there is a problem of incompatibility to be overcome. Except in the case of identical twins, 'foreign' grafts, even skin, will not 'take', and for all practical purposes, the grafts must be taken from another part of the patient's own body. Many ways of solving this problem are being explored and few would dare assert that it is insoluble. A few exceptions to this rule have been found: e.g. the cornea (the transparent covering on the front of the eye), cartilage and large arteries may be transplanted with impunity. A start was made in 1952 on a 'cornea bank' (on the lines of the blood bank) which would help to restore sight to many blind patients. In that year an Act of Parliament made it possible to 'bequeath one's eyes' for this purpose. It was found that tissues of this kind, if treated first with glycerine, may be preserved for long periods in 'deep-freeze'. It has also been found that the human body can tolerate within it some of the most useful of the modern synthetic plastics, a fact which has been used [4] to advantage in the surgery of the heart and blood vessels.

Even before man knew that blood circulated in the body, the sixteenth-century surgeon Ambroise Paré taught that the arteries should be tied off after an amputation and in the succeeding centuries this ligation of arteries and veins was employed to treat aneurysms and varicose veins. Cardiovascular surgery as we know it today really began in 1896 when J. B. Murphy, an American, succeeded for the first time in sewing together a severed artery, and Ludwig Rehn, a German, made the first successful repair to an injured heart. In this same decade several operations on the thorax were performed, but this was a dangerous procedure, for the moment the lungs are exposed to the air and its normal pressure they collapse. In 1904 the German surgeon Sauerbruch invented a 'negative pressure chamber' in which the lungs could be protected from this mishap, but this was not developed for at about the same time anaesthetists devised the endotracheal tube which provided a simpler answer to the problem. When it is inserted through the mouth and into the windpipe the anaesthetist can supply the patient's lungs with a mixture of anaesthetic gases, pure air or oxygen, at any pressure required, so permitting the surgeon to remove any diseased part of a lung or even a whole lung. This control of the patient's respiration by external means has been followed by the external control of his circulation by the 'heart-lung machine'. Instead of going through the heart, the patient's blood is circulated through this machine so that for comparatively long periods the surgeon may operate on the unmoving heart and its surrounding vessels. Congenital heart defects, which are often quite simple faults in these organs, have thus become accessible to surgery and many of the 'blue babies' born with these defects have recently been cured. The weakened and obstructed aorta which often develops with old age has also been attacked in this way, the unserviceable portion being removed and replaced by a fresh graft from the deep-freeze or by a plastic [5] substitute.

[The above passage, taken from *A Short History of Medicine* by F. N. L.

Poynter and K. D. Keele (Mills & Boon, 1961), is reproduced by kind permission of the authors and publishers.]

1  (i) Use any **five** or the following words in sentences to show that you can use them correctly:

unprecedented (1), malefactors, exponents (3a), impunity, tolerated (4), ligation, accessible (5).

(ii) Find suitable synonyms for any **five** of the following words:

attributed, accumulated (1), incompatibility, assert, insoluble, bequeath, synthetic (4).

(iii) Using your own words, explain briefly what is meant by:

(a) incendiary raids (3b)        (b) arterial aneurysms (5)
(c) cardiovascular surgery (5)    (d) an endotracheal tube (5)
(e) congenital heart defects (5).

2  (i) Construct an outline plan of the passage by choosing for it a new title, and giving suitable headings and sub-headings for its sections and sub-sections:

Title ...........................................................................................................

Section 1.......................................................................................................
„        2.......................................................................................................
„        3.......................................................................................................
              (a).........................................................................................
              (b).........................................................................................
„        4.......................................................................................................
„        5.......................................................................................................

(ii) List some of the factors that the authors suggest are mainly responsible for 'the spectacular progress which surgery has made over the last ten years'.

(iii) Although in many instances surgeons knew in theory that certain operations could be performed, they often had to wait for two things to happen before the operations were actually attempted. What were these two things?

(iv) In what field of surgery did Horsley and Cushing specialise?

(v) Under a suitable heading, summarise Section 3 in not more than **sixty-five of your own words**.

(vi) Why, according to the authors, was 'it no accident' that it was a Venetian surgeon who introduced skin grafting into Europe? Why was it in the sixteenth rather than any other century that this particular method was adopted?

(vii) Explain what the authors mean when they refer in Section 4 to 'the problem of incompatibility'.

(viii) In what important way does a corneal graft differ from a skin graft?

(ix) Place the answers to the following questions under one comprehensive heading:

(a) To what extent could it be argued that Ambroise Paré was born before his time?

(b) What factor made early operations on the thorax so dangerous? How was this danger eventually overcome?

(c) In what major way did the introduction of the 'heart-lung machine' help surgeons operate on the heart?

(d) Give a list of some of the operations that new machines and skin grafting techniques have made possible.

**RESEARCH. In each case, give the source of your information**

3  (i) Who discovered that the blood circulated within the body; in what year did he publish his findings; and what was the name of the book?

(ii) In what year, and where, did Ludwig Rehn make the first successful repair operation to the heart?

(iii) Give the dates of the Napoleonic Wars.

(iv) Write brief biographical notes on any **five** of the following:

| | |
|---|---|
| (a) Sir Victor Horsley | (b) Harvey Cushing |
| (c) Sir Harold Gillies | (d) Sir Archibald MacIndoe |
| (e) Ambroise Paré | (f) J. B. Murphy |
| (g) Ludwig Rehn | (h) Sir Peter Medawar |
| (i) Professor Christian Barnard | |

# Atomic Physics in Medicine

The application of atomic energy to weapons of destruction does not concern us here, but there are many other uses for atomic energy which do. But first we must go back a bit to that wonderful radio-active element discovered by the Curies—radium. Why was radium of such value to mankind? The secret was in those penetrating rays. In some diseases certain cells in the body grow abnormally, and these growths of unwanted cells, or cancers, may often be fatal. In certain forms of these diseases, growths are destroyed by powerful rays. X-rays, from outside the body, can sometimes have this effect, but X-rays destroy living tissue as well, and if the growth is not near the surface more harm than good may be done to the patient. But if a tiny amount of radium is inserted into the growth itself sometimes its rays will stop the growth without harming the patient. This was the great contribution radium made to
[1] medicine.

And then, with the discovery of how to split the atom in the atomic pile, it became possible to make a whole new range of radio-active materials. For if you put other elements—sodium, or phosphorus, or calcium, for example—into the atomic pile some of their atoms will capture some of the nuclear particles flying about in the pile, and new *isotopes* of these elements will be formed.

These new isotopes are radio-active. For, unlike the stable, naturally occurring one, the man-made isotope of sodium, for example, does not last for long, and its extra energy is given off in the form of penetrating rays or electrically-charged particles.

A radio-active isotope is similar in its chemical properties to the ordinary form of the element. Radio-active sodium, for instance, combined with chlorine is still sodium chloride, or common salt, and it dissolves in water and behaves in other ways just like salt made from ordinary sodium. But a radio-active substance has the advantage that it can be traced easily, for the radiation it gives out can easily be picked up and measured on an instrument known as the *Geiger-Müller* counter. It is as *tracers* that radio-active elements are largely
[2] employed in medicine. Here are some examples.

Bone consists largely of the chemical substance calcium phosphate. In order to make bone, you need to eat foods containing both calcium and phosphorus. Calcium is contained in many foods, among them milk. By making small amounts of the calcium in certain foodstuffs radio-active, and tracing, by means of a Geiger-Müller counter, the rate at which the radio-active calcium is absorbed by the body cells, it is found that of all foods milk is by far the best source of calcium for the human body, since the calcium in milk is more easily
[3] built up into bone than calcium from any other source.

One of the constituents of blood is sodium chloride, or common salt. When a surgeon is carrying out a skin graft it is important for him to know when the attached piece of skin is receiving a normal supply of blood. If he injects a little salt solution containing radio-active sodium into the patient's blood stream he can follow the course of the radio-active particles with the counter and so find [4a] out whether the skin graft has 'taken' properly.

This use of radio-active salt for tracing the course of a blood supply has had one very interesting application in the operation for separating Siamese twins. It is of enormous help to the surgeon when attempting to separate such twins, if he knows beforehand whether the two babies have blood vessels [4b] in common.

In some cases the doctor needs to know the exact volume of a patient's blood. He can draw off a small sample of the blood, 'label' some of the red blood cells with radio-active atoms of phosphorus, return the measured sample to the body, and, when it has had time to circulate and get thoroughly mixed up, draw off another measured sample of blood and find out how much the radio-activity has been diluted. A little simple arithmetic then enables him to cal- [5] culate the total volume of blood in the patient's body.

One of the most important glands in the body is the thyroid, in the neck. Sometimes a thyroid gland is over-active, sometimes it is not active enough for proper health. The thyroid gland needs iodine, and any iodine taken in by the body is, sooner or later, extracted by the thyroid. If a little radio-active iodine is introduced into the body its rate of absorption by the thyroid, measured by the Geiger-Müller counter, tells the doctor whether the thyroid is functioning properly, and, in some cases, helps to decide whether an operation is [6] necessary.

These are just a few of the many applications of radio-active substances to medicine today. Like radium, some of the new radio-active elements may have very valuable uses in the treatment of certain diseases, as well as in diagnosis. And there are other uses for them also. Germs, as well as non-living things, may be 'labelled' with radio-active elements and the history of the germs in the body may be traced. On a larger scale, outside the body, germ-carrying insects may be 'labelled'. For example, house flies have been fed on radio-active materials and then tracked with a counter; it has been found that they can travel over thirty miles, and this has an obvious bearing on the spread of [7] diseases and its possible prevention.

Every year new ways are being discovered in which the atom—the radio-active atom—can help the doctor. It is one of the most recent tools of his trade, [8] but one of rapidly-growing importance. [*slightly abridged*]

[The above passage, taken from *Science and the Doctor* by F. R. Elwell and J. M. Richardson (Bell, 1957), is reproduced by kind permission of the authors and publishers.]

1   (i) Find suitable synonyms to replace any **five** of the following words used in the passage. Use the remaining five in sentences to show that you can use them correctly:

penetrating, contribution (1), dissolves (2), absorbed (3), constituents (4a), circulate, diluted, calculate (5), extracted, absorption (6).

(ii) Write brief descriptions of the following:

    (a) Geiger–Müller counter,    (b) Siamese twins,
    (c) thyroid gland,             (d) atomic pile.

(iii) Describe the properties and uses of any **five** of the following:

    sodium, phosphorus, calcium, uranium, radium, chlorine, sodium chloride, calcium phosphate, iodine.

(iv) Comment on the authors' use of 'and', 'but' and 'for', particularly for opening sentences. Does the fact that they are used to open sentences detract from the style and meaning? Possibly you might think that they help to make the style more informal and friendly.

2  (i) X-rays are used for two main purposes: for *diagnosis* (not mentioned in the passage) and for *treatment*. Under a suitable heading, explain (a) for what type of treatment X-rays are used, and (b) mention the dangers of such treatment.

(ii) Under a suitable heading, explain:

    (a) how radio-active isotopes are made;
    (b) how these man-made isotopes differ from naturally-occurring ones; and
    (c) how they are used in medicine.

(iii) Give at least one example mentioned in the passage to show how doctors have made use of radio-active isotopes of:

    (a) calcium,          (b) sodium,
    (c) phosphorus,     (d) iodine.

    Explain the mechanics involved in each procedure.

(iv) Make a list of other uses to which radio-active tracers have been put. Can you suggest other possible uses *not* mentioned in the passage?

(v) Answer the following questions:

| | Answers |
|---|---|
| What is the chemical name for common salt? | |
| What is the name of the important bone-building chemical found in milk? | |
| Who first discovered radium? | |
| Sodium chloride consists of two elements, sodium and one other. What is the other? | |
| In medicine, radio-active isotopes are generally used as . . . | |
| What is the name of the instrument that measures intensities of radiation? | |
| In what part of the body is the thyroid gland situated? | |

RESEARCH. In each case, acknowledge the source of your information

3  (i) Make a list of as many uses to which (a) X-rays and (b) radio-active isotopes have been applied, not only in medicine but also in other fields —industry, engineering, pure science.

(ii) What precautions should be taken when using radio-therapy equipment?

(iii) In what year did Pierre and Marie Curie receive a Nobel Prize for Physics? With whom did they share it?

(iv) Complete the following table:

| Wilhelm Konrad von RÖNTGEN | 1845–1923 | Discovered X-rays |
|---|---|---|
| Marie CURIE | | |
| Pierre CURIE | | |
| Antoine Henri BECQUEREL | | |
| Hans GEIGER | | |
| Ernest RUTHERFORD | | |
| Irène JOLIOT-CURIE | | |
| Jean Frédérick JOLIOT-CURIE | | |

(v) The book from which the passage is taken was published in 1957. Suggest additions you could make to bring the passage up to date.

# Florence Nightingale:
# Her Life and Work

Florence Nightingale (1820–1910), the creator of modern nursing, was born in Florence while her parents were on a visit to Italy. She and her sister were brought up partly at Lea Hurst in Derbyshire and partly at Embley in Hampshire. Her parents were wealthy, and when young, Florence was much admired in London society for her beauty and wit. Even so, from the age of 17, she felt that she was called to serve God in a special way, and it soon [1] became clear to her that her vocation was to nurse the sick.

Her parents were horrified when she asked permission to enter a hospital for training. The hospitals of those days were filthy, fever-ridden places, and most of the nurses were ignorant and drunken. It was an unheard-of thing for an educated woman to wish to be a nurse. Florence had to give up her wish to train, and instead she did what nursing she could in the villages near her home, and studied hospital reports when she could get them. She travelled abroad with friends, visiting hospitals in many places, and in 1851 she managed to train for 3 months in a hospital run on model lines at Kaiserwerth in Germany.

When their daughter had refused a most suitable proposal of marriage for no other reason than that she meant to be a nurse, the Nightingales reluctantly accepted the fact that nothing would keep her from her career. In 1853 Florence became Lady Superintendent of the Institute of Sick Gentlewomen [2] in Harley Street, London.

In 1854 Britain was involved in the Crimean War against Russia. Horrifying reports reached England about the British Army hospital at Scutari, near Constantinople, to which thousands of sick and wounded were sent from the Crimean battlefields. The buildings were not properly equipped, and there were only untrained medical orderlies to nurse the patients. Sidney Herbert, the Secretary of State for War, an old friend of Florence Nightingale, wrote to ask her if she would take a party of nurses out to Scutari, and his letter [3] crossed with one from her offering to go.

In November, 1854, she arrived at the hospital with about thirty nurses. They found terrible conditions: there were no medicines, no beds, no bedding; the huge building was filthy, and desperately overcrowded; there was no proper drainage system, and the smell was frightful; there was no hot water. Worst of all, the doctors had no authority to make the government departments [4] provide what was needed.

Florence Nightingale was received with suspicion. Nurses were unheard of in a military hospital; the doctors thought they would only be a nuisance. But she had brought medical supplies with her, and she had at her disposal a fund of money raised by *The Times*, and she was not afraid of regulations. She provided medicines, blankets, shirts, soap, and scrubbing brushes. By her orders an entire wing of the hospital was repaired and equipped in time to receive 800 new patients. As well as carrying out her enormous task of organisation, Florence Nightingale nursed the worst cases herself. She was known to spend 24 hours at a stretch on her feet in the wards. At night she made her rounds with a lantern. The soldiers worshipped her, calling her 'The Lady with the Lamp'. The doctors now turned to her for everything they needed.

Meanwhile, the army in the Crimea was desperately short of supplies and winter clothing, and in consequence thousands of sick men poured into the hospitals. In January, 1855, there were 12,000 men in Scutari and 42 per cent of them died. Florence Nightingale's masterly organisation and determined insistence on getting her own way greatly improved conditions, and after the drainage and water supply had been attended to the death-rate began to fall
[5] immediately. By June it was only 2 per cent.

Later, Florence Nightingale travelled through the Crimea fitting out and organising hospitals. The physical strain was terrific, and she fell desperately ill; but when she recovered, though her friends urged her to go home, she insisted on returning to work. She extended her activities by providing recreation rooms, books, and lectures for the convalescents, and later for soldiers who were well. Their officers accused her of 'spoiling the brutes' but, as a result, drunkenness among the men decreased, and they began to save
[6] their pay and send home their savings through a scheme suggested by her.

When peace came in September, 1855, she did not leave Scutari until the hospital was empty. When she came home the nation longed to honour her publicly, but she would not allow it. In 1856 she was received by Queen Victoria and the Prince Consort, who were much impressed by 'her powerful clear head and simple modest manner' and by her suggestions for improving
[7a] the army hospital system.

Ill and exhausted as she was from two years of terrible strain and hardship, she yet determined to start new work—the improvement in the conditions in the army, so that the death-rate among the troops in peacetime should not be
[7b] twice the civilian rate.

Supported by the Queen, a Royal Commission with Sidney Herbert as chairman was set up to enquire into the health of the troops. Florence Nightingale worked for it night and day, collecting information and drafting plans for reform, the house in which she lived being nicknamed 'The Little War Office'. Her aunt, who lived with her, wrote, 'She alone has both the
[7c] smallest details at her finger ends and the greatest general view of the whole'.

In 1857 her health collapsed entirely, but after a short rest she was back at work again. Health, comfort, friends, were all sacrificed to her task, and when she was too ill to travel she directed reforms in hospitals and barracks all over England from her London home. Gradually many of the things she fought for were achieved. Barracks and army hospitals improved, and an Army Medical School was founded. Many army chiefs thought her ideas molly-coddling, but in 1861 the death-rate in the army had been halved. In 1861 Sidney Herbert, her faithful friend and supporter, died, worn out with over-work. His death was a severe loss; but Florence Nightingale continued to advise the army on health and sanitation, and also did a great deal of important work for Indian [8] Public Health.

In 1860 a sum of £50,000, which had been collected in gratitude for her services in the Crimea, was used to found the Nightingale Training School for Nurses attached to St. Thomas's Hospital, London. The training, which was planned by Florence Nightingale, set a new standard of discipline, good behaviour, and nursing skill. Soon hospitals all over the country were asking for Nightingale nurses, and as the years passed nursing became established as [9] an honourable profession for women of every class.

During the second half of her life Florence Nightingale was a semi-invalid, often bed-ridden for months at a time. But statesmen, nurses, and viceroys of India came to her house in South Street, Mayfair, to consult her; letters arrived from all over the world asking her advice on hospital affairs. As she grew older the desperate, often bitter, energy that had possessed her changed to serenity. She continued to work for many years, until first her eyesight faded, and then her memory. In 1907 the King awarded her the Order of Merit. Her [10] only comment was, "Too kind, too kind'. Three years later she died.

[The above passage, taken from *Great Lives*, Vol. 5 of the Oxford Junior Encyclopaedia (Clarendon Press, Oxford, 1960) is reproduced by kind permission of the publishers.]

1  (i) Find suitable synonyms for any **ten** of the following words taken from the passage, and then use the synonyms in sentences to show that you can use them correctly:

admired (1), refused, proposal, reluctantly (2), provide (4), suspicion, disposal, insistence (5), urged (6), collapsed, sacrificed (8), gratitude (9), consult, serenity (10).

(ii) Define what is meant by a *Royal Commission*.

(iii) Find out how the term 'molly-coddling' originated.

(iv) Study the spelling of the following words in readiness for a spelling test:

superintendent, nuisance, drunkenness, scheme, desperate, permission, convalescents, discipline, behaviour, honourable, profession.

2  (i) Give the passage a new title, each section an appropriate heading, and each sub-section a sub-heading. This will give you an outline plan of the passage:

Title...........................................................................................................................

Section 1...................................................................................................................

,,  2...................................................................................................................

,,  3...................................................................................................................

,,  4...................................................................................................................

,,  5...................................................................................................................

,,  6...................................................................................................................

,,  7...................................................................................................................

(7a)...................................................................................................................

Section 7    (7b)......................................................................................
             (7c).....................................................................................
   „    8.............................................................................................
   „    9.............................................................................................
   „   10...........................................................................................

(ii) From the information in the passage, make a list of the main landmarks
in Florence Nightingale's life. Base your work on the table below:

| Date | Age | Relevant information |
|------|-----|----------------------|
| 1820 |     | Born in Florence, Italy |
| 1837 | 17  | Already determined to become a nurse |
| 1851 | 31  | Three months' hospital training at Kaiserwerth, Germany |

(iii) Explain why, during the first half of the nineteenth century, it was
'unheard-of for an educated woman to wish to become a nurse'.

(iv) In what ways did Florence Nightingale show her determination to
become a nurse?

(v) From the information given in the passage, describe Scutari Military
Hospital (a) before the arrival of Florence Nightingale;
and   (b) after she had re-organised it.

(vi) Explain how Florence Nightingale became known as 'The Lady with
the Lamp'.

(vii) What facts go to prove that the officers were incorrect when they
accused Florence Nightingale of spoiling and molly-coddling the
troops?

(viii) Florence Nightingale wanted many changes made in the British Army's
attitude to medical care. To what extent was she successful?

(ix) Florence Nightingale's method of training nurses was geared to
achieving three professional characteristics. What were they?

(x) The impact made by Florence Nightingale during her own lifetime was
reflected not only in the official honours she received (the audience
with Queen Victoria and Prince Albert; the O.M. awarded to her by
Edward VII) but also by many honours of a more unofficial nature.
Make a list of as many of these as you can.

(xi) Choose up to five adjectives that you think would best describe

(a) Florence Nightingale's character;
(b) her methods; and
(c) her contribution to the nursing profession.

## DISCUSSION TOPICS

Generally speaking, as a nurse meets more and more hospital situations—not
all of them pleasant ones—there come times when she has to re-assess certain

of her moral values; traditional and accepted thinking has to be re-considered in the light of new experiences.

Now is as good a time as any to deal with some of the major controversial topics that occasionally crop up in discussion. A useful practice is to organise debates based on each of the following topics and debate them, say, one a week, with a different team preparing arguments for and against each motion.

(a) Birth control
(b) Abortion
(c) Sterilisation (particularly of the 'Unfit')
(d) Euthanasia
(e) Corporal (and/or capital) punishment
(f) Vivisection
(g) Darwinism v. the literal interpretation of the Bible
(h) Unmarried mothers
(i) Adoption
(j) Divorce
(k) Suicide
(l) Cremation
(m) State welfare
(n) Drinking/driving under the influence of drink.
(o) Smoking/lung cancer
(p) Drug addiction
(q) Conservation/Pollution.

In this country there exist many voluntary societies whose purpose is concerned with the laws relating to the subjects referred to above. Although many run on small budgets, you will find that most of them will supply on request any information you require. The addresses of many of these are to be found in the section 'Societies and Institutions' in *Whitaker's Almanack*, and in the *General Information* section of the *Daily Mail Yearbook*.

Another very useful book for the debater is *Pros and Cons* published by Routledge & Kegan Paul.

# The Background to Social Medicine

Medicine has passed through many phases from the time when disease was regarded as a punishment from the gods or a sign of devil possession to the present era, when increasingly there is a tendency to look on society as the patient. Indeed, one commonly hears doctors and sociologists talking about [1] 'the sick society'.

The early primitive stage came to an end—at least in one part of the world— when in Greece, five centuries before Christ, Hippocrates and others began to teach that all diseases were due to natural causes. But after the first ray of hope the outlook began to deteriorate when, during the Middle Ages (that is, from the fall of the Roman Empire right up to the fifteenth century), there was [2] a return to the belief in devil possession and supernatural causes.

Eighteenth-century medicine in Europe was materialistic, regarding the body as a machine. It was founded on a sort of pseudo-science—although, of course, there were always individual exceptions, physicians such as Sydenham in England, who, avoiding all theories, based their work on observation of the patient. This mechanistic approach persisted right through the nineteenth century, but medicine became more and more truly scientific, and the century saw the most rapid advances in the field ever known until our own times: the discovery of germs by Pasteur, of antiseptics to combat them by Lister, of vaccination by Jenner and anaesthetics by the American, Wells, and the Scot, Simpson. The use of the microscope by Virchow, who was a German, brought great advances in the understanding of disease, and Ehrlich, another German, conceived the idea of 'magic bullets' which would attack the germs at the root of the disease without harming the patient. But one of the greatest of all these [3] men is perhaps the least known. His name was Edwin Chadwick.

From the earliest period of recorded history human communities have been constantly ravaged by great plagues which swept over their lands year after year, killing untold millions. Such plagues are recorded in the Bible and other ancient books, but, when town life became more and more common, as during the Roman Empire and the Middle Ages in Europe, the overcrowded conditions were even more favourable to the spread of disease. The Black Death of 1348–9 wiped out almost half the population of Europe. But, even in the first quarter of the nineteenth century in London, tens of thousands died from typhus, typhoid, and smallpox—and not only these, for periodically cholera [4] would be brought into the country by travellers from abroad.

In the face of these terrible visitations the individual physician was

50

helpless. He could not treat each one of the many sick even had he known how, and Chadwick's claim to fame rests on the fact that he was the first man to think in terms of *social* control of diseases, by so dealing with their causes that they were prevented from arising at all. In order to wipe out typhoid and cholera, he argued, we must ensure clean water supplies; for these diseases are caused by germs carried in polluted water. In order to attack typhus and plague, one must get rid of the lice which carry the germs of typhus and the rat-fleas which carry the germs of plague (including, of course, the rats, [5] which, in turn, carry the fleas).

In the past, some attempts had been made to segregate the sick to prevent the spread of diseases—for example, in the case of leprosy (which, strangely enough, we now know to be less infectious than most germ-born diseases). But segregating those who are sick with typhoid or cholera is of little use if others are still drinking polluted water, just as it is of little use segregating plague cases if rats with their infected fleas are allowed to run at large. So these early attempts met with little success, due to the lack of understanding of [6] how the infections were passed on.

Chadwick was born in a Lancashire farmhouse where the children were washed every day all over, and he ruthlessly drove an obsession with cleanliness into the heads of his countrymen until, later in the century, it was possible for the German philosopher Treitschke to tell his class in Berlin: 'The English think soap is civilisation.' Although this remark was meant cynically, there is little doubt that soap, if it is not civilisation in itself, has played a greater part in making civilisation possible than many more elaborate remedies. A population riddled with chronic infectious illness has neither the time nor the energy to apply to the arts or sciences, and soap did a great [7] deal to reduce infection.

One of the first public health measures was introduced by Chadwick and others when they brought in legislation to purify the water supply of London. Previously, the citizens had used water from the Thames (they still do, but only after it has been filtered and sterilised at the waterworks!), and from filthy, refuse-laden ponds and springs. Later, Chadwick helped to found the Poor Law Commission, and produced a report in 1842, the principal suggestions of which were: a municipal water supply for all towns; scientific drainage both in town and country; and an independent health service with large powers for dealing with those who endangered the lives of others by polluting water or causing nuisances. He also proposed a national service for interment of the dead; for in those days bodies often remained for days in the over- [8] crowded homes of the poor without burial.

What has the twentieth century contributed to the concept of social health? Well, of course, there has been a great deal of legislation along the lines initiated by Chadwick to control disease, and a great many other measures have been introduced concerned with the idea of positive health—not merely preventing bad health, but trying to bring about the highest possible state of good health. Orange juice, milk, and good meals for school children have brought about a transformation in child health, which has become apparent to the least observant in the last ten or fifteen years. And the National Health Service is in [9] the direct line of descent from early nineteenth-century legislation.

But in future years it is probable that the main achievement of the twentieth century in social medicine will prove to be the extension of the term 'social

health' to cover every aspect of community life, not only in such subjects as
bodily health and its control by social means, but also such problems as mental
illness, crime, delinquency, drug addiction and so on. What we are now asking
ourselves is: how far are these problems produced by society itself, and if this
[10] is the case, how far can we go in preventing them by social means?

Social medicine takes the view that these problems can never be dealt with
solely by moralising and retribution, but only by dispassionately analysing
causes and dealing with them. In this century we have developed a social
conscience. Not always, it is true, a very well-informed social conscience, but
at least this is a good beginning. There are organisations for dealing scienti-
fically with delinquency, for dealing with problem children, for spreading
knowledge about cancer in order to show people that it can be successfully
treated if taken in time. The organisation known as 'Alcoholics Anonymous'
has, on the whole, been more successful in treating alcoholics by social means
than have any of the individual medical methods. Mental illness is also
treated by group methods, which, together with the new drugs, have revo-
lutionised the position in mental hospitals. We can well say with John
Donne, who died in 1631, that 'no man is an island . . . every man's death
diminishes me; for I am involved in mankind'. This is the attitude of twentieth-
[11] century social medicine.

[The above passage, taken from *Pears Cyclopaedia* (76th Edition) is reproduced by kind permission of the publishers, Pelham Books Ltd.]

1   (i) Write sentences to illustrate the meaning of any **ten** of the following
        words *as they are used in the passage*:

        deteriorate, supernatural (2), persisted, conceived (3), segregate,
        polluted (6), obsession, cynically, elaborate, chronic (7), purify,
        sterilised (8), initiated, apparent (9).

        Find appropriate synonyms and antonyms for any **five** of the above
        words. Give your answer in the form of a table.

    (ii) Find out the meaning and origin of the prefixes of the following words.
        Having done that write your findings in the following table, adding at
        least three examples for each prefix.

        *super*natural (2), *micro*scope (3), *pseudo*-scientific (3), *anti*septic (5),
        *trans*formation (9), *re*tribution (11)

| Prefix | Origin and meaning | Examples |
|---|---|---|
| super | | |
| micro | | |
| pseudo | | |
| anti | | |
| trans | | |
| re | | |

(iii) What are the 'magic bullets' referred to in Section 3?

(iv) Explain what John Donne meant when he wrote 'every man's death diminishes me; for I am involved in mankind'.

2  (i) Give the passage a new title, and each section an appropriate heading. This will leave you with the structural plan of the passage.

(ii) In your own words, explain what is meant by 'social medicine'; and then make a list of the benefits of effective social medicine.

(iii) In what ways did the ideas of Hippocrates differ from those prevalent during the Middle Ages?

(iv) What makes the author state that eighteenth- and nineteenth-century medicine in Europe was 'materialistic'?

(v) To what extend did Sydenham's ideas of medicine differ from those of his contemporaries.

(vi) Under a suitable heading, make a list of the major advances made in medicine during the nineteenth century.

(vii) Placing each under an appropriate heading, make a list of:

(a) the factors that made conditions favourable for epidemics in the past; and

(b) the factors that have helped to facilitate the control and prevention of these epidemics.

(viii) In what way was Edwin Chadwick's view of controlling infectious diseases fundamentally different from the ideas prevalent at the time?

(ix) Make a list of the main recommendations made by Chadwick in the 1842 Report.

(x) Summarise Section 9 in not more than **45 of your own words**.

(xi) The author believes that in time social medicine will be extended to cover many other social illnesses. What are these?

(xii) **In your own words**, explain what is meant by the first sentence of Section 11.

(xiii) To what extent is the author correct in saying that 'in this century we have developed a social conscience'?

**RESEARCH.  In each case, acknowledge the source of your information**

3  (i) Write brief biographical notes on the following:

Thomas Sydenham (1624–89)    Joseph Lister, Baron (1827–1912)
Edward Jenner (1749–1823)    Louis Pasteur (1822–95)
Edwin Chadwick (1801–90)    Sir James Young Simpson, Bart (1811–70).

(ii) Find out the address of each of the following. Having done that, choose any **one** organisation and make a list of its main aims.

(a) The Royal Society of Health
(b) Family Welfare Association
(c) National Association for Mental Health.
(d) National Marriage Guidance Council.
(e) Royal Society for the Prevention of Accidents.
(f) Alcoholics Anonymous.

(iii) Write a *specimen* letter to the secretary of the local branch of the Marriage Guidance Council inviting him to send a speaker along to talk to the class on either the aims of the Council or some particular topic in which the class is interested.

## CLASS ASSIGNMENT

It is suggested that each class member writes a short essay (300–600) words on any **one** of the following topics, the finished articles to be collected together under the title 'Communal Health'. Perhaps the class-teacher might be persuaded to write an introduction.

| | |
|---|---|
| The School Health Service | The Home Help Service |
| Maternity Services | Care of Old People |
| The Health Visitor | Mental Welfare |
| The District Nurse | Meals on Wheels Service |
| Venereal Disease (Control) | The Public Health Inspector |
| Industrial Hygiene | Immunisation and Vaccination |
| The Factory Acts | Industrial Diseases |
| The World Health Organisation | Pure Food |
| Voluntary Organisations in Social Work | Control of Infectious Diseases |
| Services for the Blind, Deaf and Disabled | Local Water Supply |

[A first-class film dealing with the work of a local authority has been made for the County Borough of Rotherham. Entitled *Rotherham Up-to-date*, it is available on request from the Town Clerk, Municipal Offices, Howard Street, Rotherham, Yorkshire. Also recommended is *The Health of a City* (B/W, 25 mins), available on hire from Films of Scotland. It deals with the history and provision of public health in Glasgow.]

# The British National Health Service

The generally accepted starting point for free health services began with the Poor Law Amendment Act of 1834, which provided free medical treatment for the sick poor. In 1912 the Liberal Government, largely through Lloyd George, introduced the National Insurance scheme. It provided, free at the time of treatment, a general practitioner service for the lower income brackets. The scheme did not provide for dependants, and offered no hospital services.

All manual and non-manual workers between the ages of 16 and 70, with an income of less than £160 a year, were entitled to benefit under what soon became known as 'the Lloyd George'. Compulsory contributions in 1912 were fixed at 3d. a week. During the 30 years of its existence, the scheme was frequently revised. The maximum income level was raised from time to time so that, by July, 1948, all earners with an income under £420 a year were [1] compulsorily insured. In all, 20,000,000 were covered.

Meanwhile, the hospital services in Britain had been developing along two broad fronts. On the one hand, there were the Voluntary Hospitals, which had their foundations in the Middle Ages: even today there are still some hospitals—like St. Thomas's and St. Bartholomew's, both in London—which were founded by monks for the treatment of the sick poor. Most of the monastic-founded hospitals crumbled away when Henry VIII purged the monasteries in Britain.

They were replaced in the early eighteenth century by what by 1900 had become known as Voluntary Hospitals. They survived simply through the generosity of local endowments. The medical staff gave their services free, but they had to be sure of attractive private practices in the neighbourhood of these hospitals to make a living.

By the early 1930s, the position had been reached where patients paid what they could afford. By then, too, local authorities were contributing something [2a] to the upkeep of these hospitals.

And around this time, a brilliant economist at the London School of Economics, Sir William Beveridge, had started to evolve the basic principles of a Welfare State. In 1942, Sir William, later Lord Beveridge, became chairman of a Government appointed committee, whose report, published that [2b] year, was the basis of the N.H.S. we have today.

By 1930, the Municipal Hospitals of Britain, whose roots were also in the Middle Ages, and which were little better than glorified workhouses, were also undergoing a social revolution: they were brought under the wing of the local authorities, and the more progressive ones—like London, Manchester, Birmingham, Middlesex and so on—started to develop them into proper hospitals, bringing them more into line with the facilities offered by the [2c] Voluntary Hospitals.

Even so, there was no real unity between the two hospital groups. The doctors in the Municipal Hospitals received a salary, but the medical staff of the Voluntary Hospitals still had to rely on private practice for a living, and by the mid-thirties private patients were becoming fewer and fewer. Worst of all, the hospitals all faced an uncertain future, relying as they did either on charity [2d] or the budgets of local authorities for survival.

The time was ripe for change. It came with the publication of the Beveridge Report. In a word, it offered—security: a comprehensive scheme for every man, woman and child in Britain to be safeguarded against financial loss through unemployment during illness or injury. It also offered radical safeguards to those who had retired.

In 1945, a year after the Beveridge Report was published, the Government accepted its principles. A year later the Government published a White Paper for a comprehensive National Health Service. The final plan was placed before Parliament in 1946. It became the National Health Service Act, which received Royal Assent on 6 November, 1946, and came into operation 19 months later [3] on 5 July, 1948.

This bold and exciting dream was summarised in the words of the Act 'to promote the establishment in England and Wales of a comprehensive Health Service designed to secure the improvement in the physical and mental health of the people of England and Wales and the prevention, diagnosis and treatment of illness'. Separate Acts were passed for Scotland and Northern Ireland, but the facilities they offered were almost identical to those in England and Wales.

[4]     Free-for-all medicine had finally arrived.

It was inevitable that since 1948 there has grown up in the public's mind a great deal of suspicion towards the N.H.S. These suspicions have been fanned in a number of quarters: phrases like 'compulsory medicine', 'lack of flexibility', 'Whitehall bureaucracy', 'socialised medicine', have been tagged to the N.H.S. It is not a bad thing, therefore, to state the basic objects of the Service as it operates today.

The very backbone of the N.H.S. is that it provides everybody in this country —irrespective of age, sex, occupation, social status—with the best medical and allied services available, to cover every possible aspect, from minor ailments to major surgery.

The N.H.S. is also available to visitors from overseas who are taken ill or sustain an accident after they have entered Britain; but overseas residents who come to this country for treatment are usually expected to pay for it.

There is no compulsion for patients to make use of the N.H.S. if they still want private treatment. Nor is any doctor forced to join the N.H.S.: in fact only 600 out of a total of 23,500 general practitioners have opted out.

But anyone may make use of the Service, either partly or entirely, and there are no insurance qualifications required; the fact that your National Insurance Card may have a number of stamps missing is no barrier from being seen by a doctor or consultant, or having an operation; but it does affect your Welfare State benefits. Another important point: the N.H.S. allows you to have a private doctor and at the same time have a bed in a State hospital—but the same patients cannot be treated privately and under the N.H.S. by the same doctor.

The N.H.S. is free, except for a few small charges—for spectacles, bifocal lenses, dental treatment and certain appliances.* But in the case of hardship and for war pensioners, refunds are available; there are also exemptions for [5] children, teenagers and expectant mothers. [*slightly abridged.*]

[The above passage, taken from *The National Health Service and You* by Gordon Thomas and Dr. Ian D. Hudson (Panther, 1965) is reproduced by the kind permission of the authors and publishers.]

1   (i)   Study the punctuation in Section 2c in readiness for a dictation test.

   (ii)  Take any five of the following words and use them in sentences so that their meaning becomes clear:

       revised (1), evolve (2b), comprehensive (4), inevitable, compulsory, opted (5).

   (iii) Write simple, but precise, definitions of each of the following terms used in the passage:

       Voluntary Hospitals, Middle Ages, endowment (2a), Welfare State (2b), Municipal Hospitals (2c).

   (iv)  To what extent is 'free for all' in the last sentence of Section 4 an unfortune choice of phrase?

2   (i)   Write a plan of the passage, by giving each section a heading and each sub-section a sub-heading.

   (ii)  To what extent are the following dates important in the history of social security in this country?

       1834, 1912, 1942, 1945, 1946, 1948.

   (iii) **In your own words**, explain 'the Lloyd George' scheme introduced in 1912.

   (iv)  Under a suitable heading, make a list of the differences that existed between the Voluntary and the Municipal Hospitals.

   (v)   **In your own words**, state the aims of the N.H.S. Act (1946).

   (vi)  Write a summary of Section 5 in not more than **sixty-five of your own words**. Place the summary under a suitable heading.

**RESEARCH.   In each case state the source of your information**

3   (i)   Write brief notes on the following Government Departments.

       (a) Environment          (b) Health and Social Security
       (c) Home Office          (d) Education and Science.

---

* On 1st April 1968, prescription charges (of 2s. 6d. per item) were re-introduced into the N.H.S. This charge was increased to 20p per item in April 1971.

(ii) Write brief biographical notes on the following:

(a) David Lloyd George, (b) Lord Beveridge, (c) Aneurin Bevan.

(iii) Write a note-form account of the Poor Law Amendment Act (1834), giving the story behind it, its provisions, and its main effects.

(iv) Construct a well-labelled diagram showing the structure and organisation of the N.H.S. in England and Wales (or Scotland).

(v) Complete the following table by inserting the cost in £millions of the N.H.S. in England and Wales, Scotland, and Northern Ireland. In brackets, give the approximate cost per head of the population in each country.

|         | England and Wales | Scotland | N. Ireland |
|---------|-------------------|----------|------------|
| 1965–6  | (    )            | (    )   | (    )     |
| 1966–7  | (    )            | (    )   | (    )     |
| 1967–8  | (    )            | (    )   | (    )     |
| 1968–9  | (    )            | (    )   | (    )     |
| 1969–70 | (    )            | (    )   | (    )     |
| 1970–71 | (    )            | (    )   | (    )     |
| 1971–2  | (    )            | (    )   | (    )     |

(vi) **In your own words,** explain the procedure for changing one's doctor.

(vii) Write an account of the Health Service as it exists in any one other European (or Commonwealth) country. It is suggested that each class member takes a different country and the resultant essays collected together under the title *The Health Services of Europe* (or *the Commonwealth*. [You will find that most foreign embassies supply information of this nature, and are particularly cooperative when requests made to them are well-written and genuine.]

# Public Health on an International Scale

The earliest recognition of the idea that public health is an international and not merely a national problem can be traced back to the fourteenth century. When the Black Death was rapidly spreading through Europe an agreement was reached by certain nations concerning primitive quarantine regulations. But it has invariably happened that when an international emergency is over, all further co-operation between the nations on the subject of health ceases. No other international collaboration of this nature seems to have taken place until 1851 when an international conference was called in Paris in order to reach some agreement on quarantine regulations in the Mediterranean and Black Sea areas. Again this proved to be only a fleeting coming-together of the nations and when agreement had been reached the committee dissolved itself.

The first permanent international body of a sanitary nature to meet was the outcome of a conference of American Republic representatives held in Washington in 1902. The object of the conference was to promote international co-operation in public health measures among the nations of the two American continents. Seven years later the field of international co-operation was widened further by the opening of an International Office of Public Health in Paris. It was intended that this body should in course of time become world-wide in scope, and forty-six countries actually joined it. The chief aim of this international body was the same as that of its predecessors, the American Sanitary Bureau, that of reaching quarantine agreements which would prevent disease being transferred from one country to another. It was not really con-
[1] cerned with the health conditions within each of the individual countries.

In 1923 the League of Nations established its Health Organisation and also made certain arrangements for attacking specific diseases on a world-wide scale. The central governing body of this organisation was the Health Committee. Under the supervising Health Committee there worked a secretariat, a staff of experts, and a number of sub-committees dealing with specific problems, such as malaria, cancer and housing. The Second World War
[2] brought to an end all these League of Nations activities.

The story of world co-operation in health problems starts again in the year 1946 when a preliminary International Conference was held in New York at which a constitution for a World Health Organisation was drawn up. The Constitution given to this World Health Organisation (W.H.O. for short) shows great breadth of vision on the part of those who devised it. Health was defined as 'a state of complete physical, mental and social well-being, and not

merely the absence of disease or infirmity'. The preamble to the Constitution also states that 'the enjoyment of the highest attainable standard of health is one of the fundamental rights of every human being, without distinction of
[3a] race, religion, political belief, economics or social condition'.
This broad statement was amplified later and the actual work of the W.H.O. brought to a clearer focus. Its function was declared to promote maternal and child welfare, and to help to improve mental health, and more especially those aspects of mental health on which harmony between human beings depends. Another part of its aims was 'to promote, in co-operation with other specialised agencies . . . the improvement of nutrition, housing, sanitation, recreation, economic or working conditions, and other aspects of environmental hygiene. . . . It was also to study and report on . . . administration and social technique, affecting public health and medical care from preventive and
[3b] curative points of view, including hospital services and social security'.
Already the W.H.O. has accomplished much for world health. It has sent its representatives into the backward countries and has assisted these countries to deal more satisfactorily with their urgent health problems. It has, for example, sent medical commissions into Asia to make frontal attacks on malaria, yaws and venereal diseases. Since the discovery of penicillin and the sulphonamide drugs, the last two of these three diseases can be brought much more quickly under control than was formerly possible and the various commissions not only supply what is required in the way of drugs and equipment but instruct the native inhabitants in their use. Much also has been done for maternal and child welfare by the W.H.O. and this has brought into prominence yet another world problem, that caused by overpopulation. The steep fall in infant mortality which has taken place both in Asia and Africa has aggravated a problem which has long existed in these continents, that of insufficient
[3c] food supply for the growing population. [*slightly abridged.*]
[The above passage, taken from Kenneth Walker's *The Story of Medicine* (Hutchinson, 1954; Grey Arrow Edition, 1959) is reproduced with the kind permission of the publishers.]

1   (i) Complete the following table by giving the origin and meaning of each word, and then finding three medical terms to illustrate the meaning of each prefix.

| Word | Meaning | Origin | Examples |
| --- | --- | --- | --- |
| international (1) | adj. between nations | inter (L.) between natio-onis (L.) —to be born | intercostal interfemoral intermaxilliary |
| Mediterranean (1)* | | | |
| promote (1) | | | |
| predecessor (1) | | | |
| transferred (1) | | | |
| supervising (2) | | | |

* N.B. Do not confuse *medius* (L. middle) with *medicus* (L.) from which *medical* is derived.

(ii) Write sentences to illustrate the meaning of any **five** of the following words:

quarantine, collaboration, prevent (1), amplified, harmony (3b), accomplished, aggravated, prominence (3c).

(iii) Give precise definitions of any **two** of the following terms:

quarantine regulations (1), environmental hygiene (3b), yaws (3c), sulphonamide drugs (3c).

(iv) Differentiate between the following pairs of words:

(a) *malnutrition* and *under-nutrition*
(b) *diagnosis* and *prognosis*
(c) *exanthem* and *enanthem*
(d) *digestion* and *absorption*.

2 (i) Construct a plan of the passage by giving each section a suitable heading and each sub-section an appropriate sub-heading. Place these under a new title of your own choosing.

Title ................................................................................................................
Section 1....................................................................................................
    ,,   2................................................................................................
    ,,   3................................................................................................
               (a)..........................................................................
               (b)..........................................................................
               (c)..........................................................................

(ii) Using a system of dates, make a note-form summary of the attempts made at international co-operation in public health up to the outbreak of World War II. Give the reasons for these attempts.

(iii) Draw a labelled diagram to illustrate the organisation of the Health Organisation of the League of Nations.

(iv) In what major respect did the International Office of Public Health and the American Bureau differ from the later international health organisations belonging to the League of Nations and the United Nations?

(v) In your own words, re-write those parts of the W.H.O.'s constitution that are quoted in Section 3a of the passage. To what extent do you think that the author is correct in stating that the W.H.O.'s constitution 'shows great breadth of vision on the part of those who devised it'?

(vi) Under a suitable heading, make a list of the functions of the W.H.O.

(vii) To what extent has the W.H.O. been successful in achieving its aims?

(viii) 'As man's knowledge of disease widens, more emphasis is placed on preventive medicine.' Explain and then discuss.

**RESEARCH.  In each case acknowledge the source of your information**

3 (i) Find out the following information about the World Health Organisation (W.H.O.):

(a) the address of its headquarters;
(b) the name of its Director-General, together with a short biography;
(c) the exact date its Constitution was adopted;
(d) its functions;
(e) the names of any major non-member nations.

Do the same for the Food and Agriculture Organisation (F.A.O.) and
the United Nations Educational, Scientific and Cultural Organisation
(U.N.E.S.C.O.).

(ii) Construct diagrams to illustrate the structure of the W.H.O., F.A.O.
and U.N.E.S.C.O.

(iii) Write an essay on the *control* of any **one** of the following:

locusts, sandflies, mosquitoes or the tsetse fly.

(iv) Find out as much as you can about the life and work of any **one** of the
following:

Sir William Boog Leishman, Sir Patrick Manson, Charles Donovan.

**ASSIGNMENT.** In this assignment, the class is set the task of producing
its own 'Handbook of Tropical Diseases'. Each individual student (or pair of
students) should choose a different disease and write an essay on it, the completed essays being collected together to form the handbook.

*Suggested plan:*
(a) Definition of the disease, and its distribution (include a map)
(b) Description of symptoms
(c) Causes
(d) Treatment
(e) Prevention/Elimination.

| | | |
|---|---|---|
| Malaria | Measles (*Morbilli*) | Kwashiorkor |
| Yellow Fever | German Measles (*Rubella*) | Beriberi |
| Sleeping Sickness | Influenza | Pellagra |
| Undulant Fever | Whooping Cough | Bacillary Dysentery |
| Endemic Syphilis | Leprosy | Amoebic Dysentery |
| Plague | Yaws | Tapeworm infections |
| Cholera | Tuberculosis | Roundworm infections |
| Kala azar | Typhus | Fluke infections |
| Enteric Fevers (Typhoid and Paratyphoid) | | |

## Part II
### REVISION NOTES AND EXERCISES

---

# The Parts of Speech

There are eight parts of speech, each with a specific job to do. The eight are as follow :

| Part | Function |
|---|---|
| 1. Nouns | give *names* to things. |
| 2. Pronouns | are used instead of nouns. |
| 3. Adjectives | describe nouns (or pronouns). |
| 4. Verbs | are words that express *action* or *being*. |
| 5. Adverbs | modify the meaning of verbs. |
| 6. Conjunctions | are 'joining' words. |
| 7. Prepositions | show the relationship between a noun and some other word in the sentence. |
| 8. Interjections | are words that are 'thrown' into a sentence to add atmosphere. |

Now let us deal with each part of speech in more detail.

**(1) NOUNS** These are *naming words*. There are five types—Common, Proper, Collective, Abstract, Verbal.

(*i*) *Common.* A common noun is a name shared by everything common to a group, e.g. girl, nurse, street, hospital, church, etc.

(*ii*) *Proper.* A proper noun is a name given to a special person, animal, place or thing, e.g. Joan, Lenny the Lion, St. Bartholomew's, St. Mary's, etc.

(*iii*) *Collective.* A collective noun gives a name to a collection of persons, places, animals or things, e.g. audience, class, flock, etc.

**N.B.** Generally, a singular collective noun takes a singular verb: e.g. The Cabinet *considers* it advisable to . . .
A set of rare old books *was destroyed* in the fire.

(*iv*) *Abstract.* An abstract noun is a name given to a state, quality or feeling, e.g. courage, love, childhood, sweetness.

(*v*) *Verbal Nouns.* These are names given to actions, e.g. swimming, walking, etc.

Examine this sentence: '*Swimming* is a good exercise.'
Here, *swimming* is a noun. It is the subject of the sentence ('is' being the verb), and can be replaced by a pronoun, in this case, 'it'.

**Exercise 1**   Make a list of at least five nouns:
   (a) used by a doctor;
   (b) worn by a nurse;
   (c) found in an operating theatre;
   (d) felt by a patient (i) before an operation, e.g. *fear* and (ii) after an operation, e.g. *relief*.

**Exercise 2**   Pick out all the nouns that appear in the following passage. In brackets after each, indicate its type, e.g. patient (common).

The patient's fear of his forthcoming operation was considered by many of the staff to be an insult to the skill of Mr. Stead and his team of cardiac specialists. Mr. Pringle's lack of courage, however, was not meant to show any lack of confidence; his feelings were highly personal and purely natural. The surgeons concerned realised the man's position, and gave the matter no more thought.

**Exercise 3**   Make a list of five collective nouns that occur frequently in hospital terminology. Use each one in singular form in a sentence to illustrate the rule that *a singular collective noun takes a singular verb.*

**(2) PRONOUNS**   Pronouns are used to replace nouns. By their use we avoid the ungainly and confusing repetition of the same nouns.
   Although there are many types of pronouns (Personal, Demonstrative, *interrogative* Emphatic, Reflexive, Relative, etc.) we need not bother ourselves too much with these or their names. What we should be able to do, however, is recognise pronouns by being aware of the work they do.
   These are examples of pronouns frequently used:

   I, me, mine; you, yours; he, she, it, him, her, his, hers, its;
   we, us, ours; they, them, theirs;
   this, that, these, those;
   myself, ourselves; yourself, yourselves; herself, himself, itself, themselves; who, whom, which, that, etc.

**N.B.**   Do not change the pronoun when it refers to the same person.
   e.g. When **one** hears of such things **you are** disheartened. (INCORRECT)
   When **one** hears of such things **one is** disheartened. (CORRECT)

**(3) ADJECTIVES**   Adjectives are *describing* words. They are used to give nouns (and pronouns) a more precise and clear definition. There are several *DESCRIPTIVE* types of adjectives (Qualitative, Quantitative, Demonstrative, Possessive, etc.) but they all have one quality in common, they *describe nouns.*
   Below is a list of examples of several different types of adjectives.
   He is *a skilful* surgeon.
   *The patient is overweight.*
   *Many* visitors arrived late.   QN
   *A large* number of nurses leave *the* profession *each* year.   DISTRIBUTIVE
   Cllr. Mrs. W. Smith has been chairman of *the* Housing Committee for *ten* years.   QU
   *An* apple *a* day keeps *the* doctor away.
   *His* impact on *the* audience was *remarkable.*
   *Her* success was due entirely to *her own* efforts.
                        EMPHASIZING

Card. Nos. 1, 2, 3 = Quantitative Adjs.
Ord. Nos. 1st, 2nd, 3rd = Demonstrative, with
this, that, these, those, a, an, the

*Adjectives and Pronouns:* In certain instances the same word may be used (both) as an adjective and a pronoun; but it should not be difficult to distinguish between the two uses. Remember: *an adjective* **describes** *a noun; a pronoun is used* **instead** *of a noun.*

| Pronoun | Adjectives |
|---|---|
| The fault is *his*. | *His* qualifications were impressive. |
| *These* are the specimens he referred to. | *These* specimens have been well chosen. |
| *What* are you doing? | *What* formula are you using? |
| He passed *her* on the corridor. | *Her* coat was too long. |

**Comparison of Adjectives**   Many adjectives describe *qualities* possessed by a noun or pronoun. It is clearly possible for a quality to be present in different proportions, or degrees.

e.g. Although Mary is *tall*, her sister is *taller*; her brother, however, is the *tallest* of the three.

We refer to these degrees—tall, taller, tallest—as *positive, comparative* and *superlative* respectively.

There are two methods of expressing the degrees of comparison. Either '-er' and '-est' are added to the positive to form the comparative and superlative cases respectively; or, where this would result in awkwardness in pronunciation, 'more' is used before the positive to make the comparative, and 'most' before the positive to form the superlative, e.g. powerful, *more* powerful and *most* powerful.

**RULE:**   When *two* qualities are being compared, the comparative is used; when *three or more*, the superlative, e.g.

He is the *more reasonable* of the *two*.
He is the *most reasonable* of the *three*.

**NOTE:**   A few adjectives have irregular forms to denote their degrees, e.g. little, less, least; bad, worse, worst; far, farther (or further*), farthest (or furthest).

\* When distance is being compared, 'farther' is the correct version, but 'further' may also be used; in other instances, 'further' is usual. On the other hand, 'farthest' is more common than 'furthest', e.g.

Peking is farther than Moscow.
Nothing could be further from the truth.
A further reason exists, etc.

**NOTE:**   Avoid constructions like 'more tidier', 'most tidiest'. THESE ARE GRAMMATICALLY INCORRECT.

**Exercise 4**   Pick out the adjectives in the following:
(a) Although forty next birthday, she has retained her youthful looks and charms.
(b) Deep X-ray treatment involves the careful use of penetrating X-rays.

(c) Radioactive isotopes are useful aids in solving many physiological and medical problems.

(d) Disposable, pre-sterilised syringes are now in regular use in British hospitals.

(e) This year forty pupil nurses joined the staff at St. Mary's Hospital.

**(4) VERBS**   A verb is a word (or group of words) that denotes the *action* done by a noun (or pronoun) or the *state of being* of that noun.

> e.g. The groundsman *cut* the lawns yesterday. (*action*)
> The surgeon *will operate* on Mr. Walker on Thursday. (*action*)
> The sample *is* here. (*being*)

A verb may denote the action (or state of being) that took place in the *past*, will take place in the *future*, or is taking place now, i.e. in the *present*. These are the three main **tenses** of the verb.

**Exercise 5**   Pick out the verbs in the following passage. In brackets after each, write its tense, e.g. contains (present).

The normal daily diet contains proteins, carbohydrates and fats in the following proportions:

> Protein, 10 to 15 per cent of the whole.
> Carbohydrate, 50 to 60 per cent of the whole.
> Fat, 30 to 35 per cent of the whole.

Where the economic situation of the family limits the buying of food it will usually be found that the carbohydrate percentage increases while the protein and fat percentage both decrease, since the main sources of these foodstuffs (meat, fish, eggs, butter, cream, milk) are relatively expensive.

It is recommended that the protein in the daily diet should average 1 gram per kilogram of body weight.

In addition to protein, carbohydrate and fats for energy, growth and repair, the body needs water, vitamins and salts. These are usually present in sufficient quantities for health in the average mixed diet and thirst is an adequate guide as a rule for the fluid intake. Although most foods contain water and some is derived from the oxidation of food within the body, an intake of at least 2 litres per day (4 pints) represents the normal requirements. (*Baillière's Pocket Book of Ward Information*, Ed. Marjorie Houghton. Baillière, Tindall & Cassell, 1965.)

**The Split Infinitive.**   The *infinitive* is that part of the verb containing 'to', e.g. to sing, to study, to have sung, to have studied. To split the unity of the infinitive is grammatically incorrect.

> e.g. The Board decided *to* finally *reject* the proposal. (INCORRECT)

*Note*:   There are occasions, however, when the split infinitive gives a smoother reading than the grammatically correct form:

> e.g. Her work as matron served *to* greatly *enhance* the name of the hospital.

**(5) ADVERBS**   It has been seen how, by adding an adjective to a noun, one is able to define the noun more clearly and precisely. In much the same way, the *action* (or state of *being*) of the verb can be modified or made more precise by the use of adverbs:

e.g. She spoke sensibly.

     verb   adverb

Although there are many types of adverbs, we will concern ourselves with only four, i.e. those telling us **how**, **when**, **where** and **why** an action took place.

(*i*) *Adverbs of Manner.* These tell us **how** an action took place, e.g. slowly, *well ill* quickly, thoroughly, gaily, stupidly, drunkenly, well, badly, delightfully. *so as* *however*

(*ii*) *Adverbs of Time.* These tell us **when** an action took place, e.g.

now, then, before, soon, late, early, yesterday, today, tomorrow, seldom, often, always, afterwards, etc. *when*

Of course, adverbs need not be single words; they may be phrases or clauses,

e.g. *Later that night,* the patient had a relapse.
     '*When I was young,* the National Health Service was a dream of the future,' said the old man.

(N.B. See the section on *Expanding the Simple Sentence,* pp. 73–75.)

(*iii*) *Adverbs of Place.* These say **where** the action took place, e.g.

here, there, above, below, under, far, near, etc. *where*

(*iv*) *Adverbs of Reason.* These tell us **why** an action took place, e.g.

'I became a nurse,' she said, '*because I considered it a worthwhile profession.*'

*Note:* The word 'not' is an adverb of negation—simply, a negative.

**Exercise 6** Pick out the adverbs in the following. In brackets after each, state its type:

(a) '*Before* I joined the hospital staff,' she said casually, 'I had always considered nursing a glamorous job.' [TIME, M, T]

(b) Once he had obtained the necessary qualifications, Dr. MacKinnon immediately handed in his notice and went to America, where he hoped for better financial rewards. [REPETITION, M, place]

(c) Because she considered it a worthwhile profession, the young woman returned to nursing after two years as a housewife.

(d) 'I acted stupidly here last night,' said the customer apologetically to the landlord. 'I must have drunk too much, too quickly.' [M, A of QUANTITY/DEGREE, MANNER]

**Comparison of Adverbs** As with adjectives, there are two ways of expressing the degree of comparison of adverbs:

(i) When the adverb ends in 'ly', 'more' is added to the positive to form the comparative, and 'most' is added to form the superlative, e.g.

Although Anne walks gracefully, Janet walks more gracefully; of the three, Mandy walks the most gracefully.

(ii) When the adverb does not end in 'ly', 'er' is added to form the comparative, and 'est' to form the superlative, e.g.

Anne works *hard*, Jean works *harder*, but Janet works the *hardest* of the three.

*Note:* The **comparative** is used when **two** are being compared; the **superlative** for **three or more**.
*Irregular:* well, better, best; badly, worse, worst; little, less, least; much, more, most.

**Exercise 7.** (See *Comparison of Adjectives*, p. 60.)
Each of the following sentences is incorrect in some way. Explain why each is incorrect, and then write out the sentence in its correct form.

(a) Of Jean and Anne, Jean is the most intelligent.
(b) 'This is the worse case I've ever seen,' said the Medical Officer.
(c) The second one was the easiest of the two papers.
(d) Of all the boys in the class, John is definitely the brighter.
(e) John is more tidier than his brother.

**(6) CONJUNCTIONS** (See *Joining Simple Sentences*, pp. 75–7.)
A conjunction is a word that joins words, phrases or clauses. There are two main types, Co-ordinating and Sub-ordinating.

(*i*) *Co-ordinating.* These join the *same* parts of speech or simple sentences of *equal value*, e.g. *and, but, for, whereas, either . . . or, neither . . . nor*, etc.

e.g. Carbohydrates *and* fats account for about 85% of our daily diet.
    *Both* penicillin *and* streptomycin are antibiotics.
    *Neither* Pritchard *nor* Jones wishes to be considered for the post.

(*ii*) *Sub-ordinating.* These join sentences of unequal value, i.e. where one depends on the other, e.g.

The patient left the hospital *before* the treatment was complete.

*Note:* These conjunctions are generally used to introduce adverbial clauses. This being so, they may be similarly classified.

*Manner (How)* . . . as, as if, as though, as . . . as, etc.
*Time (When)* . . . after, before, since, till, until, when, while, etc.
*Place (Where)* . . . where, wherever, etc.
*Reason (Why)* . . . as, because, since, etc.

**(7) PREPOSITIONS** Generally, these show the relationship between two things (nouns or pronouns) in the same sentence, e.g.

. . . the box *on* the table. . . .

By changing the preposition 'on', we change the relationship between 'the box' and 'the table', e.g. under, beside, near, behind, beneath, etc.
A preposition can, and often does, show the relationship between an action (verb) and a noun, e.g. The surgeon operated *on* the boy.
Many verbs and prepositions go together in pairs, e.g. one complains *of*, confers *with*, comments *on*, agrees *with*, protests *against*, etc.

to listen to
to look at
to watch for
wait for

*Prepositions at the end of sentences.* Grammatically, a preposition at the end of a sentence is incorrect, but current usage tends to accept the practice, particularly when it gives a better sound, e.g. to many people 'What are you waiting *for?*' sounds better than 'For what are you waiting?'

**N.B.** A preposition is a preposition only when it does the work of a preposition.

    c.g. (a) He climbed *down* the tree.
          Here 'down' relates 'climbed' to 'tree', and is therefore a preposition.

        (b) He climbed *down.* *can be BOTH .*
          Here, 'down' modifies 'climbed' and is therefore an adverb (Manner). *yes .*

**(8) INTERJECTIONS** This word comes from the Latin words *inter* (between) and *jacere* (to throw). Simply, an interjection is a word 'thrown' into a sentence to add atmosphere.
                    Each interjection is followed by an exclamation mark, e.g. Oh! Ugh! Ouch! Whow! etc.

# The Simple Sentence

A sentence is a *complete thought* expressed in words. It is divided into two parts, the SUBJECT and the PREDICATE.
**The subject** is what the sentence is about, e.g.

The doctor diagnosed the trouble immediately.

The above sentence is about *the doctor*. He is said to be the subject of the sentence. We can find the subject by asking 'Who?' or 'What?' **before** the verb, e.g.

The nurse *was studying* hard for her midwifery qualifications.

verb

Question: Who was studying? Answer: The nurse. (Subject)

The first sulphonamide compound *was introduced* in 1935.

verb

Question: What was introduced in 1935?
Answer: The first sulphonamide compound. (Subject)

**The predicate** is that part of the sentence that makes a statement about the subject, e.g. Marie Curie was awarded the Nobel Prize in 1911.

Subject          Predicate

The predicate contains the *verb* and often, but not always, an *object*. The object can be found by asking 'Whom?' or 'What?' **after** the verb, e.g.

Sir Alexander Fleming *discovered* penicillin in 1928.

verb

Question: Sir Alexander Fleming discovered *what*?
Answer: penicillin. (Object)

**N.B. (a)** Both the subject and the predicate are incomplete by themselves.
**N.B. (b)** The simple sentence contains only **one verb**.

**Exercise 1** Construct a table like the one below, and then study each of the following sentences very carefully. Having done that, insert each component part of the sentence into the appropriate column. The first one has been done for you. N.B. *Find the verb first.*

|  | PREDICATE | | |
| SUBJECT | *Verb* | *Object* | *Adverbs, telling us when, where, how or why an action took place* |
|---|---|---|---|
| (1) the doctor | returned | — | (a) Later that evening (Time)<br>(b) to the patient's home (Place)<br>(c) to administer a dose of adrenalin (Reason) |

(1) Later that evening the doctor returned to the patient's home to administer a dose of adrenalin.
(2) An hour later the nurse visited the patient to check his temperature.
(3) In 1796, Edward Jenner introduced his smallpox vaccine.
(4) Sigmund Freud was born in Moravia on 6 May, 1856.
(5) In 1900, Freud published his *Interpretation of Dreams*.
(6) Within two minutes, the dentist had extracted the offending tooth.
(7) Florey, Chain and Fleming shared the Nobel Prize for Medicine in 1945.
(8) The matron severely reprimanded the nurse for her silly behaviour.
(9) The bacteriologist studied the specimen very carefully for several minutes.
(10) The specimen was carefully studied for several minutes.

**The Indirect Object**    Consider this sentence:

The nurse gave the patient an injection.

The sentence contains two objects: (a) the thing given, *an injection*;
and (b) the person to whom the thing was given, *the patient*.

The thing given is referred to as the DIRECT OBJECT, because the action of the verb passes *directly* to it. The second object is called the INDIRECT OBJECT, because it denotes a person or thing affected *indirectly* by the action. Indirect objects are persons or things *for whom* or *to whom* an action is done, e.g.

She sent (to) him a letter.
Her boy-friend bought (for) her a gold watch for her 21st birthday.

**The Complement**    Study these two sentences:

(a) The girl saw a nurse. (b) The girl was a nurse.

In what ways do the sentences differ? Well, in (a) 'nurse' is the direct object of the verb 'saw'. 'Nurse' and 'girl' are two different persons. In (b), on the other hand, both 'nurse' and 'girl' refer to the same person. Here, 'nurse' is said to be the *complement* of 'was'. The complement may be said to complete the sense of a sentence having 'to be', 'to seem', 'to become', etc., as its main verb, e.g.

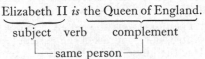

Elizabeth II *is* the Queen of England.

      subject    verb      complement

              same person

N.B. In a similar way, an adjective may complete the sense of the verb to form the predicate, e.g. The patient *is* quarrelsome.

adjective (complement)

**Exercise 2**  Pick out the objects (direct and indirect) and complements in the following sentences.

(1) Lord Lister was a great surgeon.
(2) In 1853, James Simpson administered chloroform to Queen Victoria.
(3) Adrenalin was administered to the patient.
(4) Adrenalin is a hormone.
(5) Nurse Smith wrote her mother a letter.
(6) The matron is very strict but kind.
(7) Mrs. Smith brought her son some fruit.
(8) The boy was pleased.
(9) The doctor administered the drug very carefully.
(10) The coroner's verdict was death from natural causes.

**Exercise 3**  Study the following sentences very carefully and then insert their component parts in a table based on the one below. The first one has been done for you. All *main* verbs are in italics. *Note* that in a command, the subject (You) is understood, e.g. (You) Stand up.

| SUBJECT | PREDICATE | | | |
| | *Verb* | *Object (State whether direct or indirect)* | *Complement* | *Adverb (Type)* |
|---|---|---|---|---|
| (1) the doctor | prescribed | the new drug (D) for the patient (IND) | — | later that day (Time) |

(1) Later that day, the doctor *prescribed* the new drug for the patient.
(2) British osteopaths and the B.M.A. constantly *disagree*.
(3) Gillian *approached* her examinations calmly.
(4) During her training, Nurse Smith *was* the top student two years in succession.
(5) Because she was late, she *was* not *allowed* in.
(6) Even an hour after the accident, he still *could* not *give* the policeman his name.
*(7) 'Come here,' he *said* calmly.
(8) Where *is* he *going*?
(9) Memorable *are* the days of my youth.
(10) *Boil* me this kettle of water.
(11) What a sight you *look*!

* Nos. 7–11 may be done orally, and any difficulties fully explained by the teacher.

*Note:* There are four types of sentence:

(a) *Statement*, e.g. The nurse took the patient's temperature.
(b) *Question*, e.g. Nurse, have you taken the patient's temperature?
　　　　　　　　Has the nurse taken the patient's temperature?

(c) *Command*, e.g. Nurse, take that patient's temperature.
(d) *Exclamation*, e.g. 'She's even taken the patient's temperature!' exclaimed the sister sarcastically.

*Agreement between the subject and the verb*

In grammar, the term *agreement* means that the subject and verb must agree in number and person, e.g. I *like* but she *likes*; they *like*. Rarely do difficulties arise in the general application of this rule. However, problems do occur with the use of such expressions as: *neither of, everyone, everybody, every one of, not one*, etc.

e.g. *Not one* of the students *has* passed the examination (not '*have* passed')
*None of* the passengers *was* injured in the accident. (not '*were* injured')
*Nobody is* going to remain behind.
*Everybody was* pleased with the decision. (not '*were* pleased')
At one time *anybody was* allowed to become a nurse.
*Every one of* the drivers *was* aware of the danger. (not '*were* aware')
*Every* traveller entering the city *is* searched for contraband.
*Each* of the suspects *was* questioned. (not '*were* questioned')
*Neither* Anne nor Carol *was* aware of the exam results. (not '*were* aware')
'*Either* the Secretary of State for the Social Services *or* the B.M.A. *has* spoken out of turn,' said the union official.

**Exercise 4** Delete each incorrect alternative in the following sentences:

(1) Neither of us was/were eager to come today.
(2) Everybody in the crowd was/were shouting for a quick victory.
(3) 'None of the patients in the two wards has/have a chance of a rapid recovery,' said the specialist.
(4) Neither Reynolds nor Stead has/have the necessary qualifications for the job.
(5) Not one of the nine available drugs has/have been fully approved by the Department of Health and Social Security.

## EXPANDING THE SIMPLE SENTENCE

A simple sentence is a single thought expressed in words. In its simplest form, it contains a subject and *one* verb; generally, but not always, it contains an object. A simple sentence may be expanded in two main ways:

    (a) by using *adjectives* to describe the subject and object;
and  (b) by using *adverbs* to modify the verbs.

**(a) Use of adjectives.** As subjects and objects must be nouns (or pronouns), they may be expanded by the use of adjectives. These adjectives may be single words, or phrases or clauses, e.g.

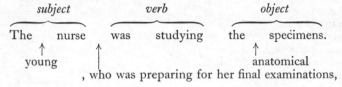

| subject | verb | object |
|---|---|---|
| The nurse | was studying | the specimens. |

young                           anatomical
, who was preparing for her final examinations,

*The* young *nurse,* who was preparing for her final examinations, *was studying the* anatomical *specimens.*

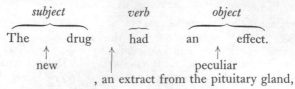

*subject*          *verb*          *object*

The      drug      had      an      effect.

↑                            ↑

new      |                peculiar

, an extract from the pituitary gland,

*The* new *drug,* an extract from the pituitary gland, *had a* peculiar *effect.*

N.B.    Nouns may be expanded by the use of *phrases in apposition.* (See *Punctuation,* p. 119.)

**(b) Use of adverbs.** (See Types of Adverbs, pp. 66–7.) Adverbs give us more information about the verb. The four main types (Manner, Time, Place and Reason) tell us how, when, where and why an action took place, e.g.

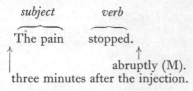

*subject*          *verb*

The pain      stopped.

↑                      ↑

|                  abruptly (M).

three minutes after the injection.

Three minutes after the injection, *the pain stopped* abruptly.

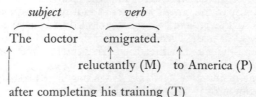

*subject*          *verb*

The   doctor      emigrated.

↑                  ↑              ↑

|              reluctantly (M)   to America (P)

after completing his training (T)

After completing his tráining, *the doctor* reluctantly *emigrated* to America.

**Exercise 5**    By using *adjectives* to describe the *nouns* (and pronouns), expand the following sentences into well balanced, easy-to-read, complex ones:

(1) The doctor married the nurse.
(2) Research appealed to the student.
(3) The hospital celebrated its centenary.
(4) Freud, Einstein and Marx were Jews.
(5) His wife visited him regularly.

**Exercise 6**    Expand the following sentences by using *adverbs* to modify the verbs.

(1) The surgeon operated on the man.
(2) Matron spoke to him.
(3) The patient laughed.
(4) The visitor gave the child fruit.
(5) The child recovered.

**Exercise 7**  By using adjectives to describe the nouns, and adverbs to modify the verbs, expand the following simple sentences. Your expanded sentences should be well-balanced, and easy to read.

*N.B.  An over-developed sentence usually sounds awkward, and is often difficult to understand.*

(1) The woman wept.
(2) The nurse gave him the drug.
(3) The workhouse became a hospital.
(4) The idea seemed strange to the politician.
(5) Salaries will be increased.

## JOINING SIMPLE SENTENCES

Like the expansion of simple sentences, joining them is a useful exercise that contributes greatly to one's skill in handling the English sentence. Of the methods used, the following two are the most frequently used.

**(a) Contraction**, i.e. reducing a sentence to a single word or short phrase, e.g.

(i) Nursing is a profession.
Nursing is *underpaid.*
Nursing is an underpaid profession.
(ii) The surgeon operated on the man's leg.
The operation was carried out *skilfully.*
Skilfully, the surgeon operated on the man's leg.
(iii) The Mayor opened the new hospital wing.
Councillor A. Briggs, J.P., was Mayor.
The Mayor, Councillor A. Briggs, J.P., opened the new hospital wing.

**(b) Conjunctions.**  (See *Parts of Speech*, p. 68.)
e.g. John signed the form.
John had read the small print.

John signed the form *after* he had read the small print.
*Before* he had read the small print, John signed the form.

Jack climbed up the hill.
Jill climbed up the hill.
Jack *and* Jill climbed up the hill.

Other conjunctions regularly used include: *but, both . . . and, for, whereas, either . . . or, neither . . . nor; after, before, when, since, till, until; where; as, because; although, though; if, unless; so that, that, in order that,* etc.

**The relative pronoun as a conjunction**

|  | People | animals/things |
|---|---|---|
| Subject | WHO | WHICH |
| Object | WHOM | |

When the noun (or pronoun) being replaced is the SUBJECT of the sentence, either 'who' or 'which' is used; 'who' is used for people, 'which' for animals and things.

When the noun (or pronoun) being replaced is the OBJECT of the sentence, either 'whom' or 'which' is used: 'whom' is used for people, 'which' for animals and things.

e.g. (i) *Subject*

This is the nurse. She was presented to the Queen last week.

*subject (person)*

This is the nurse **who** was presented to the Queen last week.

This is the specimen. It will be required for analysis.

*subject (thing)*

This is the specimen **which** will be required for analysis.

(ii) *Object*

He is the doctor. I heard him lecturing last week.

*object (person)*

He is the doctor **whom** I heard lecturing last week.

Mary found the watch. She had lost it yesterday.

*object (thing)*

Mary found the watch (which) she lost yesterday.

N.B. *Whose* is possessive, e.g.

He is a good doctor. His work is watched closely.

*possessive.*

He is a good doctor **whose** work is watched closely.

**Exercise 8** Join each of the following pairs of sentences by using *who, whom, which* or *whose*.

(1) She administered the drug. The drug was very dangerous.
(2) Nurse Jones likes reading romantic novels. Her father is a local historian.
(3) Mr. Marshall is a tradesman. He delivers groceries on Thursdays.
(4) The nurse is called Miss Matthews. She was on night duty last night.
(5) She studied the book. The book had been recommended to her.
(6) Florence Nightingale was respected by the soldiers. They called her the Lady with the Lamp.
(7) Romantic novels appeal to Miss Jones. Romantic novels tend to be like fairy tales for immature adults.
(8) He examined the man. The man had been involved in a road accident.
(9) The man was arrested by the police. They wanted him on a narcotics charge.
(10) The man escaped arrest. The police suspected him of drug peddling.

**Exercise 9** Join the sentences in each of the following pairs and groups. In each case, the sentences may be joined in a number of different ways, so experiment until you are really satisfied with the result.

(1) John left the house. It was 8.30. He intended meeting Mary at nine.
(2) William Harvey studied medicine at Cambridge and Italy. Harvey discovered the circulation of the blood.
(3) Harvey returned from Italy. He worked at St. Bartholomew's. At St. Bartholomew's he made his famous discovery. Harvey discovered the circulation of the blood.
(4) Edward Jenner was born in Berkeley. Berkeley is in Gloucestershire. He was born in 1749. He died in 1823. He studied medicine under John Hunter. Hunter was a famous eighteenth-century surgeon.
(5) Smallpox was prevalent in England. In 1796, Jenner made a discovery. Jenner found that people could be vaccinated against smallpox.
(6) Penicillin was discovered accidentally. Alexander Fleming discovered penicillin. He discovered it in 1928.
(7) The G.N.C. was established in 1919. G.N.C. stands for General Nursing Council. The address of the G.N.C. is P.O. Box 803, 23 Portland Place, W.1.
(8) The Nurses Registration Act was passed in 1919. This Act gave the G.N.C. authority to State Register suitably qualified nurses. The Nurses Act was passed in 1943. The 1943 Act gave the G.N.C. similar power to enrol nurses.
(9) Schools of Nursing offer two main courses. One course is for three years. This leads to State Registration. The other is for two years. This leads to State enrolment.
(10) The nurse successfully completed the course. The course was of three years' duration. The course led to State Registration. She was twenty-one years of age. She came from Ghana.

# The Paragraph

The purpose of paragraphing is to give the reader a rest. The writer is saying to him: 'Have you got that? If so, we'll go on to the next point.' There can be no general rule about the most suitable length for a paragraph; a succession of very short ones is as irritating as very long ones are wearisome. The paragraph is essentially a unit of thought, not of length: it must be homogeneous in subject matter and sequential in treatment.

Paragraphing is also a matter of the eye. A reader will address himself more readily to his task if he sees from the start that he will have breathing spaces from time to time than if what is before him looks like a marathon course. [*Fowler's Modern English Usage* (Second Edition), revised by Sir Ernest Gowers, Oxford University Press, 1965.]

The above passage deserves careful examination. In it, the late Sir Ernest Gowers brings our attention to four essential qualities of a good paragraph.

(a) *It must give the reader a rest*. The reader must be allowed a pause in which to assess the topic under discussion before moving on to the next. This, of course, is an essential aspect of the learning process.

(b) *It must be in sequence*. If it is to be effective, any piece of explanatory writing must give information step by step, in logical order.

(c) *It must be homogeneous*, i.e. be about one topic. All good paragraphs must have this unity.

(d) *It must help to make the completed piece of writing pleasing to the eye*. It must encourage the reader to carry on reading.

*The Short Paragraph*    Although a series of short paragraphs can be irritating, this type of paragraphing has its advantages, particularly:

(a) in business correspondence, where efficiency is considered more important than literary style;

(b) in journalism—particularly in the popular dailies—where paragraphs are often single sentences; and

(c) when writing down a conversation in Direct Speech.

The short paragraph has its advantages for the beginner, too:

(a) the writer has less opportunity to lose control over his subject matter; and

(b) he is less likely to digress into topics not concerned with the main theme.

*Qualities of a good paragraph*

(a) It must have *unity*, i.e. it must be about one subject.

(b) It should be *concise*, and not allowed to ramble out of control.

(c) It must contain a good *key sentence*.

(d) It should lead from one paragraph into the next *smoothly and effectively*.

*The Topic (or Key) Sentence* The Topic (or Key) Sentence contains the main idea of the paragraph. Generally, it introduces the subject to the reader and, like all good introductions, it should be short, clear, and to the point.

There are two main types of paragraph:

**(a) Loose** In a Loose Paragraph, the topic sentence comes first, and the rest of the paragraph expands the topic sentence or explains it in more detail.

**(b) Periodic** In this type of paragraph, the topic sentence comes last, to conclude the paragraph.

The importance of the *concluding sentence*—even in a Loose Paragraph—cannot be over-emphasised.

(a) It should bring the topic naturally to a close.

(b) It may be used to sum up the ideas expressed in the paragraph.

(c) In a complete composition, it may serve as a stepping stone to the following paragraph.

**Note:** FOR THE BEGINNER, THE BEST TYPE OF PARAGRAPH IS ONE IN WHICH THE TOPIC SENTENCE COMES FIRST, AND THE FINAL SENTENCE ACTS AS A LINK WITH THE FOLLOWING PARAGRAPH.

Study the following quotation very carefully. Obviously, the first paragraph is LOOSE, i.e. the topic sentence comes first; but notice how the concluding sentence flows so naturally into the next paragraph.

*While there are no exact figures available, there is no doubt that deafness is on the increase in this country.* The last survey into the handicap was done by the Central Office of Information in 1949; it was then estimated that 12% of the population between 65 and 74 years, and over 25% of the population over 74 years, were severely or moderately deaf. The incidence of deafness was almost nearly twice as high in the North of England, than it was in the South. The survey pointed out that although the majority of totally deaf had consulted a doctor 'sometime in their lives', only about half those suffering with less acute hearing problems had done so. *On all levels there seems to be a lingering belief that little can be done to alleviate deafness.*

The fact is that there have been a number of recent medical advances in treating certain kinds of deafness, and perseverance with treatment can often produce striking results. . . .' (*The National Health Service and You*, Gordon Thomas with Dr. Ian D. Hudson, Panther Books, 1965.)

**Exercise 1** Read the following paragraphs carefully, and then:

(a) state which is the topic sentence of each paragraph; and

(b) state the type of paragraph, i.e. Loose or Periodic.

(i) The administration of oxygen is needed in conditions where the normal supply of oxygen to the tissue cells cannot be maintained. This may be due to respiratory difficulties, circulatory failure, or to the inability of the red blood cells to combine with oxygen, as happens in the case of carbon monoxide poisoning. Examples of common conditions in which oxygen is either essential or beneficial are pneumonia, collapse of the lung (atelectasis), pulmonary emphysema, cardiac and thoracic surgical operations and congestive cardiac failure. (*Baillière's Pocket Book of Ward Information*, Baillière, Tindall & Cassell, 1965.)

(ii) Without the full co-operation of doctors, the N.H.S. would collapse today. From time to time the medical profession has used this knowledge as a means of getting concessions. Basically, though, this sort of tough bargaining is not new; it has been going on since Lloyd George introduced his National Health Insurance Bill in 1912. The opposition was determined, and at times fierce. The major line of attack from the doctors was on two broad fronts: they didn't get sufficient money from the 'Lloyd George'; they feared what one doctor has called 'the deadly hand of State Control'. (*The National Health Service and You*, Gordon Thomas, with Dr. Ian D. Hudson, Panther, 1965.)

(iii) Private patients can choose any surgeon they like to perform an operation, providing he is on the consulting staff of the hospital or clinic they are admitted to. N.H.S. patients, on the other hand, can only *ask* for a particular surgeon to perform an operation. If he is not too busy the chances are he will. If he is, he will get a senior assistant to operate. The standard of surgery amongst all the hospital medical staff is so high—due to the stringent demands of the N.H.S.—that nobody need have any fear of being operated on by an inexperienced doctor. All junior staff are closely supervised by a consultant, until they have proven their skill. (*The National Health Service and You*, Gordon Thomas, with Dr. Ian D. Hudson, Panther, 1965.)

**Exercise 2**  Use each of the following sentences as a topic sentence, first in a Loose paragraph and then in a Periodic one.

(a) The National Health Service came into operation at midnight on 5 July, 1948.

(b) Vermin thrive in dirty surroundings.

(c) A home is more than the house in which people live.

(d) Yeasts are unicellular plants of microscopic size.

(e) Nursing is now a well paid, attractive profession.

**Exercise 3**  Write a paragraph of about six well-balanced and well constructed sentences on each of the following. In each case underline the topic sentence.

(a) The qualities of a good nurse.

(b) Nursing qualifications.

(c) Training to be a nurse.

(d) The National Health Service.

(e) Love.

## Part III
## TECHNICAL WRITING

Technical writing is an acquired art and a specialised one, but the skill is not too difficult to attain. The first basic requirement is a sound *knowledge of the subject* you are writing about; the second is a reasonably good grasp of the *vocabulary* in that subject. What remains is a little formal *instruction* and, as in most things, plenty of *practice*.

# Describing Objects (instruments, tools, drugs, diseases, etc.)

*Stage I.* Every object falls into its own particular *class* or *group*. Our first task when describing anything is to place that particular object into its class, e.g.

a thermometer is a *scientific instrument*,
a scalpel is *a surgical instrument*, etc.

**Exercise 1** Complete the following table by inserting the class name of each of the objects mentioned:

| Object | Class/Group | Object | Class/Group |
|---|---|---|---|
| spoon | an eating utensil | quinine | drug |
| petrol | | phenol | |
| test tube | | phenobarbitone | |
| eye dropper | | penicillin | |
| splint | | cocaine | |

*Stage II.* The next stage in describing objects is to state the **use** of the object, e.g.   Quinine is a drug *used to reduce fever.*
A thermometer is a scientific instrument *used for measuring temperature.*

**Exercise 2** Complete the following table by stating the **class** and the **use** of each noun that appears in column one:

81

| Object | Class | Use |
|--------|-------|-----|
| cardiograph | an instrument | to measure heart movements |
| stethoscope | | |
| 'Dettol' | | |
| Streptomycin | | |
| X-rays | | |
| Higginson's | | |
| syringe | | |
| microscope | | |
| kidney | | |
| pulmometer | | |
| senna | | |

**Exercise 3**   Give brief, precise definitions of the following:

an ointment, a lozenge, a pessary, a liniment, a vaccine.

*Stage III.* Having placed the object into its *class* and stated its *use*, our next job is to make a note of the object's relevant *distinguishing features.*

*N.B. Additional Information.* Where one places additional information will depend largely on its importance. Certain by-the-way information or information that needs further explanation is best written as a footnote. Where the information is considered of the utmost importance, it may be included in the main text and, if necessary, underlined or printed in capitals.

Study the following two extracts very carefully, paying particular attention to the set out of the description.

**Penicillin**   The first and still the most widely used of the antibiotics is penicillin, produced from the mould *Penicillium notatum.*

Penicillin is effective against a number of common organisms including streptococci, staphylococci, pneumococci and gonococci. It is free from toxic side effects and can be given in very large doses, **but some people develop a sensitivity which is manifested by allergic reactions, such as urticaria and even anaphylactic shock. For this reason patients should be asked if they have had previous penicillin treatment, and if thought necessary they should be given a small test dose.** [*Baillière's Pocket Book of Ward Information.*]

**The Circulatory System**   The circulatory system is the transport system of the body by which food, oxygen, water, and other essentials are carried to the tissue cells and their waste products are carried away. It consists of three essential parts: (1) The **blood**, which is the moving vehicle by which materials are carried to and from the tissues.
(2) The **heart**, which is the driving force which propels the blood.
(3) The **blood** vessels, the routes by which the blood travels to and through the tissues.
[*Aids to Anatomy and Physiology for Nurses*, Katherine F. Armstrong, Baillière, Tindall & Cassell, 1964.]

**Exercise 4** Write descriptions of **five** of the following, attempting at least one from each section.

Section (a) streptomycin, 'Elastoplast', tuberculosis, fracture board, stomach pump, oxygen tent.

Section (b) the blood, the heart, the liver, the kidneys, air.

Section (c) preventive medicine, barrier nursing, occupational therapy.

*Stage IV.* **Describing a process.** The next stage involves yet another aspect of descriptive writing, that of describing a process. The more detailed the study, the more it becomes necessary to explain not only what the object is, but also to explain **how it works.**

Hints  (1) Be clear, precise and to the point. This means acquiring the art of choosing the right word at all times.

      (2) Give only essential information. (If you consider it necessary to add any additional information, present it at the end, preferably as a footnote. See III above.)

      (3) Present your information stage by stage, and this—if it is to be done well—means pre-planning.

      (4) If sketches or diagrams are added, make sure they are well drawn and labelled.

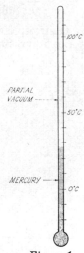

**The Thermometer**  A thermometer is a scientific instrument used for measuring temperature. It consists of a thin glass bulb from which leads a uniform capillary tube. The bulb and part of the stem contain mercury, the remaining space being a partial vacuum. As temperature rises and falls, the mercury expands and contracts, the position of the mercury thread indicating the temperature shown on the calibrated stem. (In Figure 1, it is shown in degrees centigrade.)

A clinical thermometer is one specially adapted for recording body temperature.

*Figure 1*

**Exercise 5** Write full descriptions of the following, adding well labelled diagrams where you think necessary:

a syringe, a tourniquet, a spirometer, X-ray apparatus.

**Exercise 6** Describe how any one of the following processes takes place:

(i) The digestion of food.

(ii) The circulation of blood.

(iii) The conception of a child.

**Describing diseases.**   The method employed to describe a disease is much like that used to describe an object.

*Stage I*. Place the disease into its **class**, e.g.
  Malaria is a *protozoan disease.*

*Stage II*. Attempt to give the disease a recognisable description, e.g.
  Poliomyelitis (infantile paralysis) is a *virus infection* of the nerves controlling movement, severe attacks resulting in partial or complete paralysis.

*Stage III*. Make a list of the disease's symptoms and stages in its development, explaining how—if the disease is infectious—it is transmitted from one person to another.

*Stage IV*. State the recommended method of treatment.

*Example:*   Laryngitis is a respiratory disease created by the infection of the voice-box. There is a tickling cough, and difficulty in speaking is experienced. The vocal cords are swollen and red.
  In simple cases, relief may be brought about by inhaling the vapour of Friar's Balsam (a half teaspoonful to a pint of water). If the case is serious, a doctor should be called.

**Exercise 7**   Write out full descriptions of any *five* of the following diseases:

Bronchitis, Gastritis, Haemophilia, Diabetes, Pellagra, Malaria, Tuberculosis, Scarlet Fever, Smallpox.

*infectious red patches on skin*

*a contagious feverish disease characterized by eruptions on skin*

*tendency to haemorrhage*

# Giving Instructions

The importance of giving clear instructions is nowhere more important than in the field of medicine. Here an error can—and, unfortunately, occasionally does—end in tragedy. The importance of giving clear instructions is obvious; and just as important is our ability to carry them out correctly.

When giving instructions, make sure the following 'rules' are carried out as far as possible:

(a) *Write in simple, easily understood language,* e.g.

      (i) POISON—NOT TO BE TAKEN
      (ii) Two tablets to be taken every 8 hours.

(b) *Make sure that your language fits the occasion, and is not offensive,* e.g. in a library most people would be grossly offended by a notice that read— SILENCE—AND THAT MEANS YOU!

    It must also be remembered that the wording of your instructions will depend on the person for whom the instructions are prepared. The instructions written by a pharmacist for a theatre sister are going to differ in both style and vocabulary from those given by a G.P. to an ordinary patient.

(c) *Keep your style uniform throughout.* Instructions to a friend tend to be personal in tone, containing the personal pronoun 'I'. Generally, technical instructions are written in an impersonal way.

(d) *Do not have your instructions open to misinterpretation. (Figure 2, p. 86)*

(e) *Present your information step by step, numbering each stage if necessary.*

(f) *Do not include any irrelevant information. Keep to the point.*

(g) *To give the written instructions greater clarity, add—if you consider it necessary—well labelled diagrams and sketches.*

Study the following two quotations very carefully and then complete Exercise 8 below.

### To make a Blood Smear

Place a small drop of blood on one end of a clean, polished glass slide. Then with another slide used as a spreader (held at an angle of 45° to the first, with the drop of blood in the angle between the two), allow the blood to spread across the width of the slide. Then push the spreader along the length of the slide with a firm, even motion, drawing the blood along *after* it. This should give a thin, even smear of blood on one side. The size of the drop of blood required to give a satisfactory smear can only be gauged by practice.

If an examination for malarial parasites is required, a 'thick' smear should be made. To do this, place a small drop of blood on the centre of the slide and then with the point of a needle or the end of a match smear the drop unevenly into a layer about $\frac{1}{4}$–$\frac{1}{2}$ inch in diameter. This uneven layer should be moderately thin, for if it is too thick it will flake off when being stained. (*Baillière's Pocket Book of Ward Information.*)

*Figure 2.* 'But, Martha, the instructions clearly state: "Two tablespoonfuls to be taken in water."'

## Mouth-to-Nose Resuscitation (*Figure 3, opposite*)

(1) Sweep the finger round the back of the patient's mouth to remove any obstructing matter.
(2) Grasp the patient's head with one hand and extend his neck by pressing his head backwards and at the same time lifting his jaws upwards and forwards with the other hand. Close his mouth with the thumb.
(3) Take a deep breath, place the mouth over the patient's nostrils and exhale forcibly into his lungs. Chest expansion should be observed.
(4) Withdraw the mouth and take another deep breath while the patient exhales. Repeat the cycle 10 to 12 times a minute. The first six breaths should be given as rapidly as possible.
(5) With a child his mouth and nose may be covered by the lips and the breaths should be gentler.

(*Baillière's Nurses Dictionary*, 1964, revised by Barbara F. Cape.)

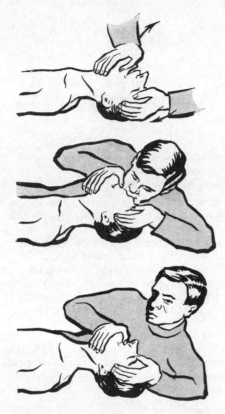

*Figure 3*. Mouth-to-nose resuscitation

**Exercise 8**   Give stage by stage instructions—including diagrams where necessary—on how you would:

(a) give mouth-to-mouth resuscitation,
(b) treat a person for shock,
(c) remove some grit from someone's eye,
(d) sterilise metal instruments,
(e) treat a chemical burn.

# Report Writing

*The child vomited a large amount of blood at 7 p.m.—mother
coming up later* [taken from *Really, Nurse!* compiled by
Roger Brook. Souvenir Press (1960), Pan Books (1966)]

Like most things, Report Writing is easy . . . once you know how. The
important thing is *method*. Once you have learnt the method, the rest is comparatively easy.

The size and type of a report will depend on many factors, particularly the
amount of information required, who wants it, and for what reasons. For
instance, a doctor's request for current information on a patient's condition
might be satisfied by a brief memo to the effect that the patient is satisfactory
and is eating regularly. On the other hand, the Ministry of Health's annual
report is a mammoth affair running into two volumes, complete with an index
and many appendices of statistics.

Nowadays, report writing for the nurse has become much easier by the
introduction of specially prepared forms that can be filled in easily. This
Proforma Reporting and the Memorandum type do not make any great strains
on the nurse. Occasionally, however, the nurse is called upon to write out
special reports relating to particular problems. It is here where skill becomes
necessary. There are two main types:

(a) the **Letter Report**, often written in the first person, i.e. using the
personal pronoun 'I'; and
(b) the **Formal Report**, often typed out and duplicated for general distribution. These can be lengthy and comprehensive in scope.

## METHOD

*Stage I.* Find out your TERMS OF REFERENCE. Except when preparing a
report for your own use, the terms of reference are generally given to you. The
instructions given to you will usually tell you:

(a) the type of information you are to collect;
(b) the amount to be presented;
(c) the type of report required (Memo, Letter, Formal); and
(d) the date by which your completed report is to be handed in.

e.g. From the M.O.H. to Administrative Officer attached to Central Clinic.

As you know, two years ago 250 infants in your area were inoculated against
measles. Please investigate the results of this experiment and report by
letter by 30 October.

88

*Stage II*. COLLECTING MATERIAL. The material you collect depends on many things, particularly: (a) the methods you use; (b) the sources of information available; (c) the time at your disposal.

N.B. Collect together only that material relevant to your terms of reference.

*Stage III*. ARRANGEMENT. Naturally, the method you use will depend on the type of report you are writing. The arrangement you choose will depend largely on your common sense. You might put your information in **chronological order**, i.e. in a time sequence. This is the method used in case histories, etc. (If you wish to read some good examples of case histories, read through some back numbers of the *Nursing Times* and *Nursing Mirror*, where you will find many reports interesting both in themselves and as examples of good technical writing.)

A report concerned with *choice*—particularly one relating to equipment or method to be employed in some scheme, say, the type of heating to be installed in a new hospital—then the method of **rejection by unsuitability** could be used to advantage. In this particular case, each type of heating would be investigated, its advantages and disadvantages considered, and the least suitable rejected one by one until the best, one hopes, would remain.

An examination of, say, the running of Regional Hospital Boards would employ a **geographical method**. On a smaller scale, the same method could be used for, say, comparing the décor of different wards in a hospital, or of different types of beds within a ward.

*Stage IV*. THE DRAFT REPORT.
Whatever the type of report used, whatever the methods used to collect, analyse and arrange information, the presentation of the report rarely varies. The structure is as follows:

(i) State your **terms of reference.**
(ii) Present your **facts.** (Supplementary evidence may be added as an appendix to your report.)
(iii) Draw your **conclusions.**
(iv) Make your **recommendations.**

N.B. (a) Do not draw conclusions that are not supported by facts.
(b) Do not let your own opinions—however strongly held—colour your judgment.
(c) Do not generalise.

**Exercise 9** Present a report on one of the following. Credit will be given for the nature of its contents, its presentation, and its general set out.

(i) Make a detailed report of the meals offered at the College or Hospital canteen over the next six weeks. Comment on the meals, and offer recommendations for improving them. Present a formal report.

(ii) Write out a report on the syllabus you are following. Suggest improvements.

(iii) Write out a report on the advantages and disadvantages of the present method of introducing young trainee nurses to hospital life.

(iv) The Regional Hospital Board intends to carry out an advertising campaign to attract school leavers into the nursing profession. It has asked you to prepare a formal report on the most effective methods to employ in such a campaign.

(v) The Hospital Management Committee is working on plans for a new nurses' home. As you, and others like you, will be living in this home, you have been asked to write to the secretary of the Hospital Management Committee offering any views you might have on the planning and the siting of the new home. You have been allowed a fortnight in which to write the letter.

# Part IV
# MEDICAL TERMINOLOGY

---

# Etymology — the sc. of origin + history of words

It is perhaps fortunate for us that the majority of medical terms are derived from Latin and Greek, languages well suited to serve this particular purpose. In fact, once one has been acquainted with the main Latin and Greek prefixes, suffixes and 'root' words used in medical terminology, one has at one's disposal the means to understand a very large number of medical terms.

The following list gives some of the main root words that nurses should find helpful in understanding medical nomenclature. (The more common prefixes and suffixes appear on pp. 93–8.)

**albus** (L.)—white, e.g. albumen, albino.
**aqua** (L.)—water, e.g. aqua bulliens—boiling water, *bullire, bulla* (L.), a bubble.
**cephale** (G.)—head, e.g. cephalagia—headache.
**chloros** (G.)—green, e.g. chlorophyll—green pigment in plants, *phyllon* (G.), leaf.
**chroma, chromatos** (G.)—colour, e.g. haemochrome—the colouring matter of blood, *haima* (G.) blood.
**chronos** (G.)—time, e.g. chronometer—an instrument for measuring time, *metron* (G.) a measure; chronic—long lasting, opposite of acute.
**coccos** (G.)—berry, e.g. streptococcus, *streptos* (G.), a chain.
**corpus, corporis** (L.)—body, e.g. corporal, corpulence.
**cutis** (L.)—skin, e.g. cutis, cuticle.
**dactylos** (G.)—finger, toe, e.g. dactylology—talking by signs made with the fingers.
**demos** (G.)—people, e.g. endemic; epidemic, *epi* (G.) among.
**dens, dentis** (L.)—tooth, e.g. dentist; dentalgia—toothache.
**derma, dermatos** (G.)—the skin, e.g. epidermis, *epi* (G.) upon; dermatitis.
**digitus** (L.)—finger, toe, e.g. digitalis—the foxglove.
**diplo** (G.)—double, e.g. diplococci—cocci occurring in pairs.
**dorsum** (L.)—posterior, dorsal, e.g. dorsomesal—lying along the middle line of the back, *mesos* (G.) middle.
**fibra** (L.)—thread, fibre.
**gamos** (G.)—marriage, e.g. polygamy, *polys* (G.) many; monogamy, *monos* (G.) one, alone.
**genos** (G.)—family, race, e.g. genetics, genus.
**glotta** (G.)—tongue, e.g. epiglottis.
**gyne, gynaecos** (G.)—woman, e.g. gynaecology.
**haima, haimatos** (G.)—blood, e.g. haemorrhage, *rhegnynai* (G.) to burst.
**homo, homeo** (G.)—same, like, e.g. homeopathy, *pathos* (G.) feeling.
**hormein** (G.)—to stir up, e.g. hormone. *homosexual*

**hymen** (G.)—membrane.
**kinema** (G.)—movement, e.g. kinaesthesia—sense of movement.
**kreas** (G.)—flesh, e.g. pancreas, *pan* (G.) all.
**malus** (L.)—bad, e.g. malformation.
**mensis** (L.)—month, e.g. menstruation.
**mnesis** (L.)—memory, e.g. amnesia, loss of memory, *a* (G.) negative.
**mors, mortis** (L.)—death, e.g. rigor mortis, *rigor* (L.) stiffness; mortality.
**narce** (G.)—torpor, e.g. narcosis, narcotic.
**nephros** (G.)—kidney, e.g. nephrectomy, nephritis.
**nervus** (L.), **neuron** (G.)—nerve, e.g. neurotic, neuritis, neuralgia.
**odous, odontos** (G.)—tooth, e.g. odontoid, resembling a tooth, *eidos* (G.), form.
**olere** (L.)—to smell, e.g. olfactory, *facere* (L.) to make.
**opsis** (G.)—sight, e.g. optic.
**os, oris** (L.)—mouth, e.g. oral.
**pepsis** (G.)—digestion, e.g. dyspeptic, *dys* (G.) bad. *Rpt e Acid*
**phobos** (G.)—fear, e.g. hydrophobia—fear of water, *hydor* (G.), water; claustrophobia—dread of confined places, *clausus, claudere* (L.), to shut.
**phren** (G.)—mind, e.g. schizophrenia—split personality, *schizein* (G.) to cleave.
**phragma** (G.)—wall, partition, e.g. diaphram.
**pneumon** (G.)—lung, e.g. pneumonia.
**polios** (G.)—grey, e.g. poliomyelitis—inflammation of the grey matter in the spine. *SPINAL*
**pulmo, pulmonis** (L.)—lung.
**rigor** (L.)—stiffness, e.g. rigor mortis.
**septikos** (G.)—putrefying, e.g. antiseptic, *anti* (G.), against.
**septum** (L.)—partition.
**scopos** (G.)—a view, e.g. stethoscope, *stethos* (G.), the breast; microscope, *mikros* (G.), small.
**soma, somatos** (G.)—a body.
**sopor** (L.)—sleep, e.g. soporific—making or causing sleep. *stupor*
**stoma, stomatos** (G.)—mouth, e.g. stomatitis, inflammation of the interior of the mouth.
**streptos** (G.)—chain, e.g. streptococcus. *berry*
**styptikos** (G.), **stypticus** (L.)—to contract, e.g. styptic.
**tachos** (G.)—speed, rapid, e.g. tachycardia—rapid heart action, *kardia* (G.), heart.

**Exercise 1** Write down *forty* examples of words, together with their meaning and origin, derived from the above Greek and Latin words. Avoid using the same 'root' word twice.

**Exercise 2** (a) The origin of each of the following terms is to be found in classical mythology. For example, the term *venereal*, ironically enough, is derived from Venus, the Roman goddess of love. Taking each term in turn, describe its origin, and comment on its significance.

aphrodisiac, atropine, hermaphrodite, hygiene, lesbian, morphia, narcissism, Oedipus complex, tendo achillis.

(b) Find out the meaning and origin of the following:

beriberi, pellagra, kala-azar, malaria, scabious, leishmaniasis.

*mnemonics are aids to memorization
eg abbreviations, patterns or rhymes.*

# Affixes: Prefixes and Suffixes

An *affix* is a letter, group of letters or a word added to an existing word to change its meaning and/or function. There are two kinds: (a) prefixes, and (b) suffixes.

(a) A **prefix** is an affix placed at the beginning of a word (*pre* is itself a prefix meaning *before*) and usually modifies the meaning of the word before which it is placed. For instance, the Latin verb *scandere* (to climb) becomes *a*scend, *re-a*scend, *con*descend, *de*scend, *trans*cend.

(b) A **suffix**, on the other hand, is a letter or group of letters added at the end of a word, usually to alter that word's grammatical function. It may, for instance, change a part of speech, e.g.

*ly* is added to adjectives to make them adverbs, e.g. quick—quickly, loving —lovingly.

N.B. When the adjective already ends in *l*, the adverb contains a *double l*, e.g. general—general*l*y, total—tota*l*ly.

Suffixes may also be used to form diminutives, e.g. *-ling* (duckling), *-let* (booklet, nervelet), *-ette* (cigarette, maisonett**e**), *-ock* (bullock).

We are now ready to deal with prefixes and suffixes in more detail. We will deal with PREFIXES first.

The following list contains the main prefixes that occur in medical terminology. Each prefix is followed by its origin, meaning, and at least one example.

**Exercise 3**   Find out the meaning of each example given in the list, e.g. 'atrophy'—without nourishment, wasting away. (You will find that the meaning of many examples will become obvious after consulting 'Etymology', pp. 91–2 and Suffixes, pp. 95–8.)

**a** (G.)—negative, e.g. atrophy.
**ambi** (L.)—on both sides, around, e.g. ambidextrous.   *ambiguous*
**amphi** (G.)—on both sides, around, e.g. amphibian.   *amphitheatre*
**ante** (L.)—before, e.g. antenatal.
**anti** (L.)—against, e.g. antiseptic.
**auto** (L.)—self, e.g. autosuggestion.
**bi** (L.)—twice, double, e.g. bifurcate. (Usually **bin** before vowels, e.g. binocular.)   *2-pronged*
**circ(um)** (L.)—round, e.g. circumcision.   *circular*
**contra** (L.)—against, e.g. contraception.
**diplo** (G.)—double, e.g. diplopia.   *diplomacy, diploma*
**duo** (L.)—two—dual.
**dys** (G.)—hard, ill, bad, e.g. dyspepsia.   *dyslexia   indigestion arising from mal functioning of stomael*
**eu** (G.)—well, e.g. euphoria.   *eulogy*
**ex** (L.)—out of, e.g. exogenous.

*derma G : skin*

93

*ego G - I*

**epi** (G.)—among, e.g. epidemic; on—epidermis.   *hypothesis = affirmation (basis)*
**extra** (L.)—outside, e.g. extragenital.   *hypostasis (standing)*
**hyper** (G.)—many, in excess, e.g. hypertrophy. *hypertension*
**hypo** (G.)—under, e.g. hypodermic. *under skin / layers ordous*
**intra** (L.)—within, e.g. intravenous.
**mega** (G.)—large, e.g. megacolon. *megalith megalosaurus*
**meta** (G.)—change, e.g. metamorphism.
**micro** (G.)—small, e.g. microscopic.
**mis** (Eng.)—wrongly, e.g. miscarriage.
**mono** (G.)—one, e.g. monoplegia. *plegia = stroke : paralysis of 1 limb*
**pan** (G.)—all, e.g. pancreas, panacea. *universal remedy*
**para** (G.)—changed, e.g. paratyphoid.
**pen** (L.)—almost, e.g. penultimate, leuco*pen*ia.
**peri** (G.)—around, e.g. pericardium. *perimeter*
**poly** (G.)—many, e.g. polydactylism. *polymous*
**post** (L.)—after, behind, e.g. post mortem.
**pre** (L.)—before, e.g. premedication. *prefix preferred*
**pro** (G.)—before, e.g. prodromal.
**re** (L.)—again, e.g. recurrent.
**retro** (L.)—backwards, e.g. retrogression.
**sub** (L.)—under, submucous.
**super** (L.)—above, e.g. supervirulent.
**supra** (L.)—above, e.g. suprarenal. *synonym synopsis syntax*
**syn** (G.)—together, with, e.g. synthesis. *- building up of a complex whole (also gamy)*
**trans** (L.) across, through, e.g. transection.

**Exercise 4**   Find at least one extra example for each of the prefixes in the above list.

**Exercise 5**   Complete the table below by inserting appropriate examples in the blank spaces.

### CARDINAL NUMBERS

|          | Greek  | Example    | Latin   | Example                          |
|----------|--------|------------|---------|----------------------------------|
| one      | mono-  | monocular  | uni-    | unilateral (on one side only)    |
| two      | di-    |            | bi-     |                                  |
| three    | tri-   |            | ter-    |                                  |
| four     | tetr-  |            | quadr-  |                                  |
| five     | pent-  |            | quinqu- |                                  |
| six      | hex-   |            | sex-    |                                  |
| seven    | hept-  |            | sept-   |                                  |
| eight    | oct-   |            | oct-    |                                  |
| ten      | dec-   |            | decem-  |                                  |
| hundred  | hect-  |            | cent-   |                                  |
| thousand | kilo-  | kilogram*  | milli-  | milligram (1/1,000 of a gramme)  |
| half     | hemi-  |            | semi-   |                                  |

* One thousand grammes.

Now we come to a more detailed study of the **suffix**. To many students, this presents more difficulty than the study of the prefix, mainly because the function of the suffix is a little less obvious and a little more varied.

**Suffixes** may be used to:

(a) *indicate a part of speech*. Words ending in *-hood, -ship,* or *-ness* are generally abstract nouns, e.g. childhood, darkness, happiness, drunkenness, apprenticeship.
Words ending in *-ous, -eous, -acious, -ious, -icious, -itious* are generally adjectives.

**Exercise 6** Give *two* examples for each of the above suffixes.

(b) *form diminutives*, e.g. drop*let*, cigar*ette*.
(c) *form feminine forms*, e.g. wait*ress*, act*ress*.
(d) *indicate skills*, e.g. craftsman*ship*; *status*, e.g. head*ship*, lecture*ship*; and *occupation*, e.g. labour*er*, doct*or*.
(e) *indicate a state or feeling*, e.g. grati*tude*, inepti*tude*.

## AND THERE ARE MANY, MANY MORE!

**-able**, being a living suffix, may be added to any transitive verb (i.e. one requiring an object) to form an adjective.

N.B. If the verb ends in a silent 'e', then the 'e' is retained after a 'soft' 'c' or 'g', e.g. marriageable, serviceable, manageable, noticeable.
The 'e' is generally dropped after a consonant, e.g. usable, likable, describable.
Verbs ending in 'y' preceded by a consonant, change 'y' to 'i', e.g. justify—justifiable; pity—pitiable.
If a vowel comes before the 'y', then the 'y' is retained, e.g. enjoyable, payable.
Adjectives formed by adding the suffix **-ful** to abstract nouns contain a single 'l'. This, however, becomes a double 'l' when the suffix **-ly** is also added to form an adverb, e.g.

> wonder, wonderful, wonderfully;
> beauty, beautiful, beautifully.

There remain to be considered several suffixes that play a significant part in medical terminology. These, practically all of which are of Greek origin, are widely used in the descriptive naming of many diseases, conditions and types of treatment. They are used to name medical apparatus, fields of study, and many processes met in the medical world generally.

**(1) -OLOGY** This is derived from the Greek word *logia* (discourse) or *logos* (knowledge). When used as a suffix, it generally indicates a field of study, a science. For example, dermatology (*derma, dermatos*, G., the skin) is the study, or science, of the skin. A dermato*logist* is a person who studies or practises dermatology.
Look up a list of the subjects studied at, say, a medical school and you will come across what seems to be a never-ending list of words ending in *ology*. Some are self-explanatory, like bacteriology, the study of bacteria, or biology, the study of life (*bios*, G., life); others you will come to know through constant repetition, such as gynaecology (*gyne*, G., woman), mycology, the study of fungi (*mykes*, G., mushroom); others are best learnt by getting acquainted with the etymology, e.g. odontology, from the Greek *odous, odontos*, a tooth.

*horoscope    G hora: season, hour; G skopos : observe*
*horology*
*horography } art of constructing clocks*

Of the following two lists of sciences ending in *ology*, the first should be self-explanatory. Those in the second list are less commonly known.

**List I.** bacteriology, biology, cardiology, craniology, dermatology, embryology, enzymology, gynaecology, haematology, histology, laryngology, microbiology, skeletology, symptomatology, urinology, parasitology, psychopathology, physiology, radiology.

**List II.** aetiology, arthrology, ecology, endemeology, gastrology, helcology, helminthology, hymenology, hysterology, hepatology, myology, mycology, neurology, neuropathology, osteology, ophthalmology, otology, pathology, phlebology, pharmacology, rhinology, sitology, splenology, threpsology, trichology, tocology, toxicology.

**Exercise 7**   Take each word in List II and, having found out its meaning and origin, insert the information in a table based on that below.

| Word | Meaning | Origin |
|------|---------|--------|
| cardiology | a study of the heart | G. *kardia*, the heart |
| haematology | a branch of physiology dealing with the blood | G. *haima*, blood |

**(2) -GRAPH, -GRAPHY, -GRAM**   These come from the Greek *graphe*, a writing, or *graphein*, to write.

(a) **-graphy.** When used as a suffix, this generally means a description, e.g. cardiography, is derived from the *kardia* (G.) heart, and means a description of the heart.

**Exercise 8**   Find out the meaning and origin of the following:

semeiography, histography, myography, odontography, nosography.

(b) **-graph.** This generally indicates a piece of writing, or an instrument capable of writing or recording data. A cardiograph is an instrument for measuring heart beats.

**Exercise 9**   Find out the meaning and origin of the following:

kymograph, thermograph, sphygmograph, phrenograph, radiograph.

(c) **-gram.** This indicates something drawn or written; a record or graph from a recording apparatus, e.g. a diagram (*dia*, G., around) is an outline drawing, whereas a thermogram is a record taken from a thermograph.

**Exercise 10**   Name the instruments from which the following are taken:

seismogram, barogram, cardiogram.

**(3) -METER,** from the Greek *metron*, a measure, usually denotes a measuring instrument, e.g. stethometer (*stethos*, G., chest) is an instrument for measuring the chest during respiration.

**Exercise 11**   Write down the meaning and origin of the following terms:

audiometer, lactometer, pulmometer, rheometer, urinometer.

**(4) -THERAPY**  This comes from the Greek word *therapeuein*, to heal. As a suffix it means 'the art of healing by', e.g. phototherapy (*phos, photos*, G., light) is the art of healing by means of light rays, used particularly for skin diseases.

**Exercise 12**  In tabular form, write down the meaning and origin of the following terms:

hydrotherapy, physiotherapy, chemotherapy, radiotherapy, psychotherapy.

**(5) -PATHY,** from *pathos*, G., feeling, denotes a disease or its treatment, e.g. neuropathy (*neuron*, G., nerve)—any nervous disease; homeopathy (*homoios*, G., like)—a method of curing disease by giving the patient drugs that give symptoms like the disease.

The suffix *pathy* is also used to express feeling, e.g. sympathy (*syn*, G., with), with feeling, compassion; apathy (*a*, G., negative) without feeling, unconcerned).

**Exercise 13**  Give the meaning and origin of the following:

allopathy, enteropathy, osteopathy, neuropathy, psychopathy.

**(6) -TROPHY,** from *trophe*, G., nourishment, is used as a suffix to denote growth or nourishment, e.g. atrophy (*a*, G., negative) means without nourishment, a wasting away; hypertrophy (hyper, G., above) is the excessive growth of an organ.

**(7) -PHOBIA** (*phobos*, G., fear) is a suffix denoting a morbid fear or hatred of something, e.g. hydrophobia (*hydor*, G., water) is a dread of water, a symptom of rabies.

**Exercise 14**  Give the meaning and origin of the following:

agrophobia, Anglophobia, claustrophobia, negrophobia, nosophobia.

**(8) -MANIA** (*mania*, G., madness) is used as a suffix to show special types of mental derangements, obsessions, etc., e.g. kleptomania (*kleptein*, G., to steal); dipsomania (*dipsa*, G., thirst) a craving for alcohol.

**(9) -TOMY** (*tome*, G., cutting) indicates a simple cutting or cutting into, e.g. nephrotomy (*nephros*, G., kidney) an incision into the kidney.

**Exercise 15**  Give the meaning and origin of the following:

embryotomy, hysterotomy, neurotomy, phlebotomy, tenotomy, varicotomy.

**(10) -ECTOMY** (*ek*, G., out; *tome*; cutting) means to cut out, or remove, e.g. nephrectomy (*nephros*, G., kidney)—the removal of a kidney.

**Exercise 16**  Give the meaning and origin of the following:

hysterectomy, neurectomy, laryngectomy, enterectomy.

**(11) -IFORM** (*forma*, L., shape) in the shape of, e.g. cuneiform (*cuneus*, L., wedge)—wedgelike; unciform (*uncus*, L., hook)—hooklike; uniform (*unus*, L., one)—one form, one shape.

**(12) -OID** (*eidos*, G., form) in the form of, like, resembling, e.g. deltoid (Greek letter, *delta*, *Δ*) triangular shaped; anthropoid (*anthropos*, G., man)

man-like, applied to the higher apes; nephroid (*nephros*, G., kidney)—
kidney-shaped.

**(13) -ITIS.** This, appended to the name of an organ (or its root form),
invariably indicates inflammation, e.g. appendicitis, inflammation of the
vermiform appendix.

**Exercise 17**   Give the names of the organs with which the following are
connected:

carditis, bronchitis, laryngitis, uteritis, peritonitis, duodenitis, rhinitis,
enteritis, phlebitis, nephritis, cystitis, parotitis.

**(14) -AEMIA** (*haima*, G., blood) e.g. toxaemia (*toxikon*, G., arrow poison)—
blood poisoning.

**Exercise 18.**   Give the meaning and origin of the following:

leukaemia, anaemia, septicaemia, bacteraemia, hydraemia.

—OSIS  denoting condition of
                 byssinosis

# Prescriptions and Treatment Sheets

A prescription falls into four sections:

(1) the *Superscription*, consisting of the ancient symbol ℞, meaning 'take';
(2) the *Inscription*, which gives the ingredients and their qualities;
(3) the *Subscription*, containing the directions the pharmacist has to follow; and
(4) the *Signature*, often written in English, that gives the directions to the patient.

The directions that a doctor writes on a prescription come under two general headings:

(a) the instructions to the pharmacist, telling him what to prepare;
and (b) further instructions that the pharmacist has to pass on to the patient. Often, the pharmacist—writing his instructions on a *treatment sheet* —passes this information on to the nurse, who then takes on the responsibility of administering the prescribed treatment.

For the keen trainee nurse wishing to learn the abbreviations used on prescriptions and treatment sheets, a method worth adopting is first to classify each abbreviation according to its function and then to get acquainted with several specimen prescriptions. At the end of this chapter, sample treatment sheets and prescriptions will be set for translation.

## INSTRUCTIONS TO THE PHARMACIST

| Abbreviation | Latin | English |
|---|---|---|
| ℞ | recipe | take |
| f. or ft. | fiat | let it be made |
| m. or M. | misce | mix |
| mit. | mitte | send |
| N.B. | nota bene | note well |
| sig. | signetur (or signentur) | let it be labelled. |
| sec. art. | secundem artem | with pharmaceutical skill, i.e. giving the pharmacist a 'free hand'. |
| pro infans. | | for a child |

## INSTRUCTIONS TO THE PATIENT (or to the nurse)

(a) *What to take, administer or use*

| aq. | aqua | water |
|---|---|---|
| aq. dest. | aqua destillata | distilled water |
| aq. ster. | aqua sterilisata | sterile water |
| aurist | auristellae | ear drops |
| emp. | emplastrum | a plaster |
| ex. aq. | ex aqua | in water |
| ext. | extractum | extract |
| garg. | gargarisma | gargle |
| gutt. | gutta (pl. guttae) | drop |
| haust. | haustus | a draught |
| lot. | lotio | lotion |
| m. or mist. | mistura | mixture |
| narist. | naristella | nasal drops |
| oc. | oculentum | eye ointment |
| pulv. | pulvis | powder |
| suppos. | suppositoria | suppositories |
| syr. | syrupus | syrup |
| ung. | ungentum | ointment |
| tab. | tabletta (or tabella) | tablet |
| troch. | trochiscus | lozenge |
| tr. or tinct. | tinctura | tincture, solution in alcohol |

(b) *How much to take*

| aa. | ana | of each, i.e. in equal parts |
|---|---|---|
| ad lib. | ad libitum | to the desired amount |
| p.d. | pro dosi | for a dose |
| rep. | repetatur | repeat |
| ss. or fs. | semi | half |
| q.s. | quantum sufficit | a sufficient quantity |
| ut. dict. | ut dictum | as directed |

(c) *When and how to take (or administer)*

| a.c. | ante cibum | before food |
|---|---|---|
| p.c. | post cibum | after food |
| b.d. (B.D.) or b.i.d. | bis in die | twice a day |
| o.m. | omni mane | every morning |
| nocte | nocte | at night |
| o.n. | omni nocte | every night |
| p.r.n.* | pro re nata | whenever necessary |
| q.d. or q.i.d. | quater in die | four times a day |
| o.q.h. | omni quartis horis | every four hours |
| t.d.s. | ter die sumendum | to be taken three times a day |
| t.i.d. | ter in die | three times a day |
| s.o.s.* | si opus sit | if necessary |
| stat. | statim | immediately |

* Attention is drawn to these two abbreviations (p.r.n. and s.o.s.) only to condemn their use. Although still used by many doctors, the practice is condemned by the nursing profession generally, for it takes the responsibility away from the doctor and places

it on the nurse. There are instances, particularly when dangerous drugs have to be administered, when the nurse has insufficient medical knowledge to act on her own initiative.

Although the *British Pharmacopoeia* recommended as far back as 1932 that in prescription writing weights and volumes should be written in English rather than the archaic apothecaries' symbols, and that Arabic numerals replace the Roman, the tradition has been slow to die among doctors, particularly among general practitioners. Fortunately for the nurse, though, most hospitals have now not only adopted the metric system, but also have discontinued the use of Latin abbreviations on their treatment sheets. A number of enlightened ones have gone a step further, and maintain that to avoid confusion, information on treatment sheets should be written in full, in English, *preferably printed.*

## Roman Numerals

While the use of Roman numerals still persists in certain quarters, one should at least be acquainted with their use. The basic letters are as follows:

$$i = 1; v = 5; x = 10; l = 50; c = 100; d = 500; m = 1,000$$

The last three—although often used in capital letters to denote dates, e.g. MCMLXIX = 1969—are not required in medicine. This is because Roman numerals are used only for apothecaries' measures, and for these we need not go above 59. (60 minims = 1 fluid ounce; 60 grains = 1 drachm.)

The system works by addition and subtraction, i.e. by *adding* all figures that appear *after* a main figure, and *subtracting* those *before*, e.g.

$$vii = 5 + 1 + 1 = 7; xxix = 10 + 10 + (10 - 1) = 29; liv = 50 + (5 - 1) = 54.$$

The only fraction catered for in the Roman system of numbers is that of $\frac{1}{2}$, which is written as 'ss' or 'fs'.

**Revision exercise.** (Refer any queries to your teacher.)

(a) Convert each of the following into Arabic numerals:

|         |         |         |          |          |
|---------|---------|---------|----------|----------|
| (a) iv  | (b) vii | (c) ix  | (d) ifs  | (e) xviii |
| (f) xiv | (g) xl  | (h) iiss | (i) xxxvi | (j) iij  |
| (k) viiss | (l) lx | (m) xxiv | (n) ii  | (o) lviii |

(b) Convert the following into Roman numerals:

|         |         |                    |          |          |
|---------|---------|--------------------|----------|----------|
| (a) 5   | (b) 7   | (c) $1\frac{1}{2}$ | (d) 12   | (e) 15   |
| (f) 18  | (g) 24  | (h) 30             | (i) 36   | (j) 40   |
| (k) 42  | (l) 48  | (m) $3\frac{1}{2}$ | (n) 59   | (o) $7\frac{1}{2}$ |

## The Metric System

The metric system is an internationally known system of measuring weights, volumes and distances (lengths) in multiples of ten. Originating in France, and introduced there at the time of the French Revolution, it did not find general acceptance in this country until recent years. In fact, although it is comforting to note that the *British Pharmacopoeia* now uses the metric system for all drug doses, many general practitioners still use the out-dated apothecaries' measurements and Roman numerals.

We need not go into the metric system in detail here, but we should know the following abbreviations and what they stand for:

| Distance | mm for millimetre | 1,000 mm = 1 metre |
|---|---|---|
| (length) | cm for centimetre | 10 mm = 1 cm |
| | m for metre | 1,000 m = 1 kilometre |
| | km for kilometre | |
| Weight | mg for milligram | 1,000 mg = 1 gramme |
| | g (or G) for gramme | 1,000 G = 1 kilogram |
| | kg for kilogram | |
| Volume | ml. for millilitre | 1,000 ml. = 1 litre |
| | l. for litre | |

**N.B.**   Although 1 ml. = 1 cc. (cubic centimetre) it is the former that is used in medicine.

The prefix *mega* denotes a multiple of one million; and micro, 1 millionth part, e.g. microgram $(\mu g) = 1/1000$ mg or $= 0.000001$ g.

**Exercise**   Using a suitable nurses' dictionary or ward handbook to obtain any information not given in the preceding pages (e.g. *Mist. Pot. Brom.* = Potassium Bromide mixture, or *Linct. Scill. Opiat* = Gee's Linctus) translate the following instructions taken from prescriptions and treatment sheets.

*Example (a)*   Caps. Ampicillin 1 G daily.
          Translation: 1 four times a day, 1 tablet being equal to 0·25 G.

*Example (b)*   Tab. Digoxin 0·25 mg b.d.
          Translation: 1 tablet Digoxin twice a day.

   (i) Chlorothiazide, 1 G daily.
  (ii) Injection Penicillin 1 Mega Unit b.d.
 (iii) Phenindione 250 mg stat; then 25 mg t.d.s.
 (iv) Injection Streptomycin ½ G, 8 hourly.
  (v) Injection Morphine Sulph. 10 mg.
 (vi) Aminophylline suppos. 0·36 G b.d.
(vii) Adrenaline Inj. 1 in 1000. 0·5 ml. s.o.s.
(viii) Benylin Expect. 10 ml. 4 hourly.
 (ix) Mist. Potassium Citrate 30 ml. 4 hrs ex. aqua.
  (x) Inj. Hydrocortisone 100 mg 6 hrly.

*Example (c)*
R (make)
Mist. Mag. Trisil Co. (Mixture of Magnesium Trisilicate compound)
Mitte 300 ml. (Send 300 millilitres),
Sig. 15 ml. t.d.s. (Label: 15 millilitres, i.e. approx one tablespoonful, to be taken three times a day.)

The following are reproductions of common prescriptions. Examine them carefully, and then as far as is possible translate them into ordinary everyday language.

   (xi) R  Mist. Acid Acetylsal pro. inf.
           mitte 150 ml.
           Sig. 4 ml. o.q.h.

(xii) ℞ Tab. Saluric (Chlorothiazide)
    mitte xl.
    i.b.d. alt. die.

(xiii) ℞ Ung Synalar
    mitte 30 G
    Apply m et n.

(xiv) ℞ Guttae Sulphacetamide 10%
    mitte 15 ml.
    Use ii drops in R. eye 4 hrly.

(xv) ℞ Narist Sulfex
    mitte 15 ml.
    Sig. ii drops in each nostril b.d.

(xvi) ℞ Tab. A.P.C.
    mitte c
    Sig. i s.o.s.

(xvii) ℞ Cap. Pentobarbitone 100 mg.
    mitte xviii
    Sig. i or ii nocte.

(xviii) ℞ Lotion Hydrocortisone
    mitte 15 ml.
    Apply q.i.d.

(xix) ℞ Mist Amman Chlor. et Morph.
    mitte 300 ml.
    Sig. 15 ml. q.d.s. p.r.n.

(xx) ℞ Troch Benzocaine Co.
    mitte 20
    Suck 1 p.r.n.

# Part V
# SOME SPELLING AIDS

The few simple 'rules' and aids given on the following pages will not make the student a perfect speller, but they will help him to improve his spelling. Besides learning the rules and putting them into practice, one's acquaintance with words will become more intimate only through lots of reading—not merely reading to extract the content of a passage, but making a conscious effort to be aware of the words themselves. As a last resort, one can learn to spell by the old-fashioned, but often effective method of rote learning lists of selected difficult words. There are also on the market nowadays some very useful programmed spelling manuals.

## CONTENTS
 (1) **ie** or **ei**
 (2) **a** or **an**
 (3) **-ise** or **-ize** verb endings.
 (4) **-ise** or **-ice**—verb or noun.
 (5) **our** or **or**
 (6) **-ible** and **-able** endings.
 (7) Some troublesome double consonants.
 (8) Forming plurals.
 (9) (i) Homophones (ii) Homonyms (iii) Words confusingly alike.
(10) Spelling Bees.

 (1) **ie** or **ei**   **Rule:** When the sound is **ee**
                          Write **i** before **e,**
                          Except after **c.**

    e.g. **ie** words: believe, belief, handkerchief, priest, hygiene, niece, piece, achieve, grief, grieve.

     **ei** words: receipt, receive, conceive, ceiling.

     **Exceptions:** seize, seizure, weird;
               either, neither, protein, caffeine, casein, cuneiform.

N.B. Many **ei** and **ie** words do not come under this rule because they are **not pronounced with the 'ee' sound.** One is advised to learn the following:

    (a) **ei** words: neighbour, weigh, weight, forfeit, freight, vein, veil, reign, foreign, heir, heiress, height, leisure.

    (b) **ie** words: lieutenant, friend, sieve, mischief, patient, serviette, gaiety.

(2) **a or an   Rule:** Use **a** before a consonant and **an** before a vowel. This is so well known that it is hardly worth repeating. What cause difficulty are the exceptions to the rule.

(i) **a or an before u   Rule:** When the **u** is pronounced as in *uncle* or *umbilical* or *unconscious* then **an** is used; when the sound is as in *unicellular, union,* or *university,* then **a** is used.

e.g. a unit, a unique operation, a useful purpose, a urine sample, a uterus; an undeveloped film, an ulcer, an unacknowledged letter.

(ii) **a or an before h.   Rule:** Use **an** before **silent h** followed by a vowel; when the **h** is sounded, use **a**.

e.g. an habitual drinker, an honest person, an hour; a haemorrhage, a hospital, a hydrate.

(3) **-ise** *and* **-ize** *verb* **endings.** There are definite reasons why some verbs should be spelt **-ise** and others **-ize,** but they are reasons that the ordinary person finds difficult to appreciate. The list below contains some of the more important words that *must* take the **-ise** form. The bulk of the remaining words take **-ize.** In the *Chambers's Twentieth Century Dictionary,* both forms are given.

| | | | |
|---|---|---|---|
| advertise | demise | practise | revise |
| advise | despise | exercise | supervise |
| chastise | devise | improvise | surmise |
| circumcise | enfranchise | incise | surprise |
| compromise | disfranchise | promise | televise |

**As -ise is required in some words and both forms find general acceptance in others, the logical practice is to use -ise in all cases**

*New verbs in -ize.* This practice of forming new verbs by adding the suffix *-ize* to either nouns or adjectives is of American origin.

e.g. hospitalize, finalize, pressurize, moisturize, institutionalize, tenderize

Whether these words will in time take the *-ise* ending will depend largely on usage. Probably *-ise* will become the accepted form. After all, it's much easier to remember.

**Exercise 1**   (a) Make a list of at least *ten* new verbs ending in *-ize.*
(b) Compose a list of new *-ize* verbs (of your own invention if you wish) that you think would be useful in nursing.

(4) **-ise** *and* **-ice**—*verbs or nouns?*   Where a word has an *-ise* and *-ice* ending, it is generally the case that the verb takes **s** and the noun takes **c**.

e.g. to advise (v), advice (n); to practise (v), practice (n), to devise (v), device (n); to prophesy (v), prophecy (n).

N.B. to license (v), licence (n)—Chambers's gives the **c** form for both the noun and the verb.

(5) **-our** *or* **-or.** The American practice is to use **-or** in all instances. In English usage, there are no definite rules; but two trends are noticeable.

(i) The **u** is dropped in adjectives ending in *-ous* and in verbs ending in *-ise* (or *-ize*).

(ii) The **u** is generally retained in derivatives ending in *-ite* and *-able*.

e.g. vigour (vigorous), rigour (rigorous), odour (odorous, de-odorise), vapour (vaporous, vaporise), honour (honourable), favour (favourable, favourite).

(6) **-ible** *and* **-able** *endings* Unless one is an expert in Etymology (i.e. the derivation of words) there is no easy way to find out which words end in *-ible* and which in *-able*. Instead, the student is advised to acquaint himself with the following lists of useful, frequently used words ending in *-ible* and *-able*.

**-able endings.** Words ending in silent **e** generally drop the **e** when *-able* is added.

| | | |
|---|---|---|
| advisable | indispensable | rat(e)able |
| believable | irreconcilable | receivable |
| debatable | lik(e)able | reconcilable |
| excusable | lovable | removable |
| forgivable | measurable | unmistakable |
| immovable | movable | unshakeable |
| inflatable | palatable | usable |

N.B. If *-able* is added to a soft **c** or **g**, then the silent **e** is retained, e.g. changeable, knowledgeable, manageable, noticeable, peaceable, serviceable.

**-ible endings.** The following list contains the more commonly used words ending in *-ible*.

| | | |
|---|---|---|
| accessible | eligible | negligible |
| audible | feasible | ostensible |
| collapsible | flexible | permissible |
| compatible | gullible | plausible |
| credible | incomprehensible | reversible |
| discernible | indelible | tangible |
| divisible | irresistible | visible |
| edible | legible | |

(7) **Some troublesome double consonants**

(i) *adding the suffix ly.* The suffix *ly* has the function of changing an adjective into an adverb, e.g. quick*ly*, slow*ly*, thorough*ly*. When the adjective already ends in *l*, the adverb has a *double l*, e.g. gradua*lly*, emotiona*lly*, tota*lly*, usua*lly*, fata*lly*, menta*lly*. When the suffix *ful* is added to a noun, the resultant adjective has *one l*. Only when the additional *ly* is added, is the *l* doubled, e.g. beauty—beautiful—beautifully: harm—harmful—harmfully.

(ii) *adding the suffix -ness.* When *-ness* is added to a word already ending in *n*, the new word has a *double n*, e.g. drunken—drunkenness; sudden—

suddenness. The same applies to: lean, clean, mean, keen, green, sullen, open, outspoken, barren, rotten, plain, thin, stubborn, brown.

(iii) *mis- beginnings.* The prefix *mis-* means *wrongly*, as in *mistake, miscarriage, misbehave.* When added to a word beginning with s, both s's are retained, e.g. mi*ss*pell, mi*ss*hape.

(iv) *dis- beginnings.* The rule for *dis-* is the same as for *mis-*; i.e. when added to a word beginning with s, the two s's are used, e.g. disappoint, disinfect, dislocate *but* di*ss*atisfaction, di*ss*imilar, di*ss*ociate.

(v) *in- beginnings* (also *ir-, il-, im-*) The prefix *in* means *not*, as in *insane, infertile, inactive, inarticulate.*

When used with a word beginning with n, both n's are used, e.g. i*nn*ocuous, i*nn*umerable.

N.B. (a) *in* changes to *il* before words beginning with l, e.g. i*ll*egible, i*ll*egal, i*ll*egitimate, i*ll*iberal, i*ll*iterate, i*ll*ogical, etc.

(b) *in* changes to *im* before words beginning with m or p, e.g. i*mm*aterial, i*mm*ortal, i*mm*ovable, i*mm*oral; impatient, impartial, impenetrable, impenitent, impotent.

(c) *in* changes to *r* before words beginning with r, e.g. i*rr*elevant, i*rr*ational, i*rr*esistible, i*rr*egular, i*rr*elevant, i*rr*esponsible, i*rr*eligious.

(vi) *over- beginnings.* If the prefix *over* is added to a word already beginning with r, then two r's are used, e.g. ove*rr*ide, ove*rr*each, ove*rr*ate, ove*rr*efined, ove*rr*ipe, ove*rr*un.

(vii) *-ing and -ed endings.* When the suffix *-ing* or *-ed* are added to words of more than one syllable, the final consonant is doubled if:

(a) the stress, or accent, falls on the last syllable; and
(b) the last consonant follows a vowel, e.g.

|            |             |                              |
|------------|-------------|------------------------------|
| al-lot'    | allotted    | allotting                    |
| com-pel'   | compelled   | compelling                   |
| dis-til'   | distilled   | distilling                   |
| oc-cur'    | occurred    | occurring                    |
| o-mit'     | omitted     | omitting                     |
| pre-fer'   | preferred   | preferring (but pref'erence) |
| re-fer'    | referred    | referring (but ref'erence)   |
| trans-fer' | transferred | transferring (but trans'ference) |

N.B.
|           |            |             |
|-----------|------------|-------------|
| la'-bel   | labelled   | labelling   |
| quar'-rel | quarrelled | quarrelling |

**Note:** credited, benefited, benefiting, profited, accredited, blanketed, fidgeted, fidgeting, focus(s)ed, focusing, gossiped, gossiping, initialed, initialing, vomited, vomiting.

## (8) Forming plurals

(i) The usual method of forming plurals in English is by adding s, e.g. ankle—ankles, bandage—bandages.

(ii) The plural of words ending in s, x, sh and ch are formed by adding es, e.g. glass—glasses, gas—gases, bus—buses; tax—taxes, sex—sexes (but ox—oxen); brush—brushes; stitch—stitches.

(iii) Plurals of words ending in *o*. There are no definite rules here, but the following may act as guides:

(a) The usual method is by the addition of *es*, e.g. cargoes, tomatoes, potatoes, negroes.

(b) If the letter before the *o* is a vowel, then add *s*, e.g. radios, rodeos, studios, ratios.

(c) *s* is also added to a series of words found in the Fine Arts, particularly Music, e.g. altos, cantos; words still considered foreign, e.g. octavos; abbreviated words ending in *o*, e.g. pianos, stereos, photos.

**Exercise 2**   Give the plurals of the following words:

> echo       albino      portfolio   mosquito
> embryo    dynamo    soprano    stiletto

(iv) Plurals of words ending in *y*. Two rules apply here.

(a) If the letter before the *y* is a vowel, add *s*, e.g. boys, alloys, trolleys, journeys.

(b) If the letter before the *y* is a consonant, replace the *y* by *ies*, e.g. counties, countries, difficulties, majorities.

**Exercise 3**   Give the plurals of the following words:

> convoy, curiosity, pulley, kidney, fatality, chimney, storey, jersey, quality, technicality, cavity.

(v) Medical terminology abounds in words of foreign origin, and generally these words retain their original plural forms.

**Exercise 4**   (a) Fill in the blank spaces in the table below by supplying the appropriate singular and plural forms; and
(b) Where possible, write a 'rule' for each group of words.

| Singular | Plural | Rule |
|----------|--------|------|
| axis | | |
| | bases | |
| | analyses | |
| thesis | | |
| minimum | | |
| | maxima | |
| | errata | |
| stratum | | |
| calculus | | |
| | fungi | |
| radius | | |
| nucleus | | |

**Exercise 5**
Complete the following table by inserting the appropriate singular and plural forms

| Singular | Plural | Singular | Plural |
|---|---|---|---|
| chrysalis | | | criteria |
| coagulum | | | hypotheses |
| apex | | | genera |
| bronchus | | | data |
| synopsis | | | laminae |
| formula | | | crises |
| fungus | | | miasmata |
| matrix | | | media |
| sanatorium | | | stimuli |

(vi) *Compound words*. If the word is hyphenated, the plural is formed by adding *s* to the most important word, e.g. son*s*-in-law, sheath-filter*s*. N.B. The plural of *spoonful* (used as a measure) is *spoonfuls*.

**Exercise 6**   Give the plurals of the following words:

plate-culture, daughter-in-law, doctor-in-charge, cupful, handful.

(vii) *Nouns ending in f or fe*. The usual method is to change the *f* or *fe* to *ves*, e.g. knife—knives, life—lives, half—halves. The main **exceptions** to this rule are: beliefs, briefs, chiefs, roofs, proofs, dwarfs.

N.B. Words ending in *ff* generally add *s* to form their plurals, e.g. handcuffs, midriffs, skiffs. **Exception:** staff—staves or staffs. Some *f* endings take both forms, e.g. wharfs, wharves; scarfs, scarves; hoofs, hooves.

(viii) Many English words have the same singular and plural form. These are **either** (a) names of game, fish, birds and animals, e.g. salmon, trout, grouse, deer, **or** (b) words that have no 'singular' form, e.g. scissors, trousers, measles, mumps, etc.

(9) (i) **Homophones**   For our purpose, *homophones* may be defined as words that *sound* alike whether spelt the same or not—but have different meanings. For the person who finds spelling difficult they are a constant source of irritation and confusion. In the English language, there are over a thousand pairs of homophones, the more common of which have been included in the following exercise.

**Exercise 7**   Write sentences to illustrate the meaning of the following pairs and groups of homophones.

1. *allowed* (permitted), *aloud* (spoke); 2. *alms* (charity), *arms* (limbs, weapons); 3. *assent* (agree), *ascent* (climb); 4. *bare* (naked), *bear* (carry, animal); 5. *berth* (sleeping place), *birth* (born); 6. *born* (birth), *borne* (carried); 7. *brake* (stop), *break* (destroy); 8. *berry* (fruit), *bury* (inter): 9. *bread* (to eat), *bred* (brought up); 10. *buy* (purchase), *by* (near), *bye* (sport, cheerio); 11. *check* (stop), *cheque* (money); 12. *chord* (music, geometry), *cord* (string).

13. *cite* (quote), *site* (position), *sight* (eye); 14. *coarse* (rough), *course* (way); 15. *cereal* (food), *serial* (series); 16. *complement* (completes), *compliment* (praise); 17. *discussed* (debated), *disgust* (ill feeling); 18. *draft* (to draw up), *draught* (drink, air); 19. *faint* (swoon, indistinct), *feint* (pretend); 20. *flew* (did fly), *flu* (influenza), *flue* (chimney); 21. *lessen* (to decrease), lesson (at school); 22. *lumber* (wood), *lumbar* (of body); 23. *guessed* (did guess), *guest* (visitor); 24. *heal* (cure), *heel* (of foot).

25. *hear* (listen), *here* (this place); 26. *naval* (navy), *navel* (of body); 27. *muscle* (of body), *mussel* (shellfish); 28. *pain* (suffering), *pane* (window); 29. *peace* (quiet), *piece* (portion); 30. *passed* (gone by), *past* (in time); 31. *patients* (people), *patience* (forbearance); 32. *potion* (dose), *portion* (part); 33. *right* (opposite of wrong), *rite* (ceremony), *wright* (maker), *write* (words); 34. *scene* (view), *seen* (with eye); 35. *stair* (steps), *stare* (gaze); 36. *stalk* (hunt, of plant), *stork* (bird).

37. *story* (tale), *storey* (of building); 38. *their* (belonging to them), *they're* (they are), *there* (in that place); 39. *tear* (cry), *tier* (level); 40. *tire* (to lack energy), *tyre* (of wheel); 41. *vain* (proud), *vein* (blood vessel), *vane* (weather); 42. *waist* (of body), *waste* (surplus); 43. *ware* (goods), *wear* (clothes, verb), *where* (place), *were* (past tense of 'are'); 44. *wait* (remain), *weight* (heaviness); 45. *weak* (feeble), *week* (seven days); 46. *weather* (climate), *whether* (if), *wether* (ram); 47. *wretch* (unfortunate person), *retch* (vomit); 48. *mucus* (secretion), *mucous* (adjective).

**Exercise 8**    Make a list of at least **ten** homophones not listed above.

(9) (ii) **Homonyms**    For our purpose, *homonyms* may be considered as words with the same spelling but different meaning, e.g.

*sage*, wise person and *sage*, the herb;
*ref'use* (noun), waste and *re-fusé* (verb), to decline.

**Exercise 9**    Write sentences to illustrate at least two meanings of each of the following words:

permit, concert, minute, refuse, desert, inter, cat, convict, August (august), Pole (pole), reject.

**Exercise 10**    Make a list of at least five homonyms not given above.

(9) (iii) **Words confusingly alike**    These words generally cause confusion because, although having different meanings, they look and sound confusingly alike. They are not spelt alike (as are homonyms) or pronounced alike (as are homophones).

**Exercise 11**    Write sentences to illustrate the different meanings of the words in the following pairs and groups.

1. *accept* (to receive), *except* (omit); 2. *acne* (pimply skin), *acme* (crisis); 3. *adapt* (adjust), *adept* (skilful), *adopt* (take in); 4. *affect* (verb), *effect* (noun); 5. *assent* (agree), *ascent* (rise), *accent* (speech); 6. *biannual* (twice a year), *biennial* (every two years); 7. *calendar* (time), *colander* (strainer); 8. *callous*

(lacking emotion), *callus* (hard skin); 9. *deceased* (dead), *diseased* (ill); 10. *descent* (fall), *decent* (good) 11. *elude* (escape), *allude* (refer); 12. *eminent* (well known), *imminent* (about to happen); 13. *human* (of man), *humane* (compassionate); 14. *insane* (mad), *inane* (pointless); 15. *moral* (ethical), *morale* (spirit); 16. *personal* (private), *personnel* (people); 17. *recipe* (prescription), *receipt* (statement); 18. *stationary* (fixed), *stationery* (paper); 19. *suit* (of clothes), *suite* (furniture, rooms); 20. *vacation* (holiday), *vocation* (calling, work).

(10) **Spelling Bees.** The following 40 spelling exercises contain a large selection of words frequently misspelt by nurses. Many of the words— particularly the awkward ones—are repeated, often more than once.

*Suggested approach*

(i) At the beginning of the session, split the class into a number of teams. If it is considered necessary, change the teams, say, every six weeks or so.

(ii) Give the tests in sequence, so that students—possibly without prompt- ing—might take the opportunity to learn each group of words in ad- vance.

(iii) Let each team mark an opposing team's papers. On having the papers returned, each student should correct his own errors.

| Week 1 | Week 2 | Week 3 | Week 4 |
|---|---|---|---|
| camphor | bilious | corporal | steroids |
| whooping-cough | muscle | mercury | quinine |
| neutralize (or ise) | rheumatic | enamelling | rhubarb |
| surgeon | malady | disinfectant | poliomyelitis |
| etiquette | serviette | supplement | vestibule |
| thermometer | parquet | spasmodic | emulsion |
| gaberdine | receipt | abdomen | accident |
| catalogue | lozenge | abscess | college |
| tweezers | tissue | liquorice | hysteria |
| accommodate | haemorrhage | lingerie | maintenance |

| 5 | 6 | 7 | 8 |
|---|---|---|---|
| suppurate | flannelette | disinfectant | eucalyptus |
| pneumonia | maxillae | cereal | raspberry |
| denture | lingerie | miniature | adenoids |
| eucalyptus | eczema | intoxicant | diagnosis |
| pumice | adolescent | portmanteau | alcohol |
| glucose | vinegar | chlorinated | balsam |
| refrigerator | syphon | vaccine | molecular |
| nicotine | phlebitis | tonsils | inoculate |
| magnesia | cellophane | haemorrhage | specimen |
| lesion | nausea | skeleton | syndrome |
| plague | quarantine | strait jacket | superficial |

| 9 | 10 | 11 | 12 |
|---|---|---|---|
| colander | miniature | verdigris | febrile |
| adolescent | peroxide | alcoholic | prevalence |
| phial | diagnosis | protoplasm | cellophane |
| diabetes | melancholy | dispensary | obituary |
| camphorated | hypnotic | tincture | vivacious |
| escalator | memorandum | molecular | oedema |
| obituary | miasma | protein | epilepsy |
| jaundice | aerated | larynx | nausea |
| surgery | mortgage | recurrence | synthetic |
| phosphorus | regrettable | susceptible | tongue |

| 13 | 14 | 15 | 16 |
|---|---|---|---|
| glycerine | calory (or ie) | tincture | dermatitis |
| sanatorium | osteopath | jaundice | saccharine |
| mucous (adj.) | larynx | technician | glycerine |
| inhalation | caffeine | bifocal | osteopath |
| peroxide | hallucination | superannuate | therapeutic |
| sulphuric | halitosis | diaphragm | forceps |
| virulence | emaciated | dysentery | liquorice |
| syringe | inertia | welfare | conceive |
| vacuum | well-being | stamina | drunkenness |
| silhouette | phenobarbitone | phagocytes | haemoglobin |

| 17 | 18 | 19 | 20 |
|---|---|---|---|
| technician | prehensile | caffeine | laryngitis |
| psychic | laryngitis | chromosome | methylated |
| asthmatic | aerated | potassium | therapeutic |
| mucous (adj.) | corpuscle | peristalsis | biceps |
| synagogue | desiccated | saccharine | euthanasia |
| lymph | cranial | tetanus | pituitary |
| calamine | polypus | tonsillitis | procedure |
| psychosomatic | flatulence | bacillus | streptococcus |
| porous | bacillus | immigrant | maintenance |
| tetanus | dangerous | emigrant | isotopes |

| 21 | 22 | 23 | 24 |
|---|---|---|---|
| asthmatic | psychic | tonsillitis | anaesthetist |
| winceyette | flatulence | chromosome | orthopaedic |
| methylated | autopsy | salmonella | psychology |
| anaesthetist | orthopaedic | pituitary | gangrene |
| analgesic | catarrh | adrenalin | goitre |
| gynaecology | mastoid | aggravate | aperture |
| accumulate | epiglottis | atrophy | changeable |
| analyse | audible | auxiliary | chiropody |
| bulbous | circuit | cautery | stimulus |
| sinus | sulphonamides | callus (hard skin) | callous (ill feeling) |

| 25 | 26 | 27 | 28 |
|---|---|---|---|
| autopsy | stethoscope | catarrh | ammonia |
| psychiatrist | pulmonary | adrenalin | aspirin |
| gynaecologist | phlegm | goitre | broccoli |
| cyanide | apprentice | desperate | hysteria |
| gelatinous | benefited | separate | sedative |
| lacquer | hydraulic | collar | derivative |
| courtesy | diarrhoea | Mohammedan | favourite |
| syringe | kindergarten | imbecile | detergent |
| hybrid | impermeable | recurrence | physically |
| epiglottis | miscellaneous | scheme | streptomycin |

| 29 | 30 | 31 | 32 |
|---|---|---|---|
| septicaemia | fahrenheit | Mohammedan | infectious |
| diarrhoea | misshapen | generally | immaterial |
| electrolysis | digestible | sympathetic | electrolytes |
| inertia | negligible | haemorrhage | illegible |
| carbon tetrachloride | skilful | dormitory | aggravated |
| diphtheria | facilitate | imbecile | fahrenheit |
| fluorescent | government | suture | synthetic |
| appendectomy | aortic | isolate | parasite |
| euphoria | irregular | chlorophyll | vomited |
| poultice | amnesia | laryngitis | recurrent |

| 33 | 34 | 35 | 36 |
|---|---|---|---|
| dyspepsia | asylum | chromosomes | cellophane |
| alcoholic | emigrant | tonsils | desiccated |
| saccharine | incision | orthopaedic | staphylococcal |
| facilitate | asthmatic | flatulence | bilious |
| goitre | diphtheria | accumulate | technique |
| gonorrhoea | enamelled | fluorescent | auxiliary |
| obesity | syphilis | fatigue | ancillary |
| peristalsis | transferred | haemophilia | circuit |
| tendon | behaviour | mucus (secretion) | procedure |
| transference | benign | laryngitis | therapeutic |

| 37 | 38 | 39 | 40 |
|---|---|---|---|
| accommodation | chemotherapy | phenacetin | immigrant |
| recommend | pharynx | schizophrenia | antenatal |
| septicaemia | pollution | occupants | ophthalmic |
| immunisation | achievement | dyspepsia | convalescent |
| vaccination | deodorant | profession | dilution |
| inoculate | epistaxis | chronic | catarrh |
| cessation | perichondrium | quarantine | maintain |
| gynaecology | pronounce | eucalyptus | maintenance |
| posthumous | pronunciation | pituitary | eczema |
| tranquillisers (izers) | suppository | hydrochloric | varicose |

# Part VI
# PUNCTUATION

Speech is so natural that when one talks one does not stop to think about such things as capital letters, commas and the like. One speaks, and that's an end to it! When one writes, though, difficulties present themselves, particularly with punctuation. The author vividly recalls a remark made by one of his English teachers at school: 'Punctuation attempts to do for writing what expression does for speech.' How right he was!

Although some people disagree on the use of certain punctuation marks, there is sufficient comformity in this field of English for a list of acceptable rules to be drawn up.

The punctuation marks we will deal with are as follows:

| | |
|---|---|
| (I) Capital letters | (VI) Question mark |
| (II) Full-stop | (VII) Exclamation mark |
| (III) Comma | (VIII) Hyphen |
| (IV) Semi-colon | (IX) Inverted commas |
| (V) Colon | (X) Apostrophe |

**(I) CAPITAL LETTERS**  The main uses of capital letters are as follows:

(1)  **to open sentences;**

(2)  **to open each new line of poetry,**  e.g.

> 'The doctors found, when she was dead,—
> Her last disorder mortal.'—Oliver Goldsmith (1728–74).

(Many modern poets disregard this 'rule' so frequently that the day when it was one of the unalterable tenets of poetry has long passed.)

(3)  **to open direct quotations** (See *Quotation Marks*, pp. 125–7.)

> e.g. Mark Twain once wrote: 'The only way to keep your health is to eat what you don't want, drink what you don't like, and do what you'd rather not.'

(4)  **for proper nouns** (i.e. names of people, places and special things)

> e.g. Ronald Ross, London, St. Bartholomew's, Roll of Nurses.

(5)  **for adjectives derived from proper nouns,** e.g. British, Welsh, Victorian, Napoleonic.

> N.B. *plaster of paris, brussels sprouts, cardigan, pasteurise, french windows.*

(6)  **for days of the week, months, religious festivals, special secular events and periods in history.** e.g. Monday, November, Easter, Christmas Day, Middle Ages, etc.

(7)  **for titles** (together with indications of position, status and office)

e.g. Councillor John Hughes, J.P., Chairman of Seaville District Council.
Professor Sir Hedley Atkins, K.B.E., President of the Royal College of Surgeons of England
The Rt. Hon. Sir Keith Joseph, Bt., M.P., Secretary of State for Social Services.

(8) **for names of associations and societies,** e.g. General Nursing Council for England and Wales, The National Association of State Enrolled Nurses.

(9) **for denominations and political parties,**

e.g. Baptist, Congregational, Nonconformist, Anglican, Protestant, Catholic, Labour, Liberal, Conservative. One refers to the Cabinet, the Speaker, an Act of Parliament, the Houses of Parliament, the House of Commons, Department of Health and Social Security.

N.B. One refers to 'a government' but 'the Government', to 'a parliament' but 'the British Parliament'.
If a prefix is hyphenated to a proper noun, the prefix is not capitalised, e.g. anti-Communist, pro-American, un-English.

(10) **for compass points** when they refer to recognised territories or geographical areas, e.g. East Anglia, the West Country, the East (Communist) as opposed to the West (Capitalist), East Germany, Middle East, Far East, South East Metropolitan Regional Hospital Board.

N.B. The hiking party took a northerly route over the Yorkshire Moors.

(11) **for trade names,** e.g. Hovis, Horlicks, Ovaltine, Complan, Disprin, Drapoline, Bic pens, Ford Escort estate cars. Trade names are often enclosed in inverted commas or are underlined; in print they are frequently italicised:

e.g. The patient was advised to take 'Complan' during convalescence.
According to the advertisement, 'delicious, nourishing *Ovaltine* helps you keep bright and mentally alert'.

(For reasons best known to themselves and their advertising agents, more and more firms are now marketing their products under trade names that do not contain capital letters, e.g. 'vesagex' (antiseptic ointment).

**Exercise 1**   Find at least five examples of trade names that do **not** contain capital letters.

(12) **for important words in the titles of books, films, radio and TV programmes,** etc. Titles may be written in several ways, e.g.

(a) enclosed in inverted commas, e.g. 'The Golden Age of Surgery in England';
(b) underlined, e.g. Man's Anatomy, Physiology and Health;

(c) written in capital letters, e.g. PRINCIPLES OF GENETICS;
(d) in italics, the general practice in print, e.g. *Aids to Personal and Community Health.*

(13) **for the Deity.** When reference is made to the Deity, even pronouns are in capitals, e.g.

'O, God, Thou art generous and merciful.'

(14) **for the personal pronoun 'I'** (but not 'me', unless it refers to the Deity), e.g.

'My tutor told me to work harder,' said the student nurse.
**but**  'Thou shalt have no other god before Me.'

(15) **for exclamations,** e.g. Oh! Eh! Ugh!

**(II) THE FULL-STOP**  It is one thing to say that one of the main uses of the full-stop is to end a sentence; it is another to put it into practice. Many people do not know when a sentence does, in fact, end (see pp. 70–8). Besides closing sentences, however, the full-stop has other uses.

(1) **Initials, Abbreviations and Contractions** are generally, but not always, followed by full-stops.

A *contraction* is a word that has been shortened by the omission of middle letters, e.g. D(octo)r; whereas an *abbreviation* is one that has been shortened by omitting final letters, e.g. Rev(erend) or Capt(ain). *Initials* are obvious.

Today, in this age of *initialese*, it is becoming ever more difficult to read any publication without coming up against examples of initials being used instead of the full name:

S.E.N., S.R.N., T.U.C.,\* G.N.C., E.T.U.,\* M.O.H., B.M.A.,\* N.H.S., D.P.H., Q.A.s, G.C.E.,\* C.S.E.,\* B.B.C.,\* I.T.A.,\* M.P.,\* J.P.,\* H.M.I.

A practice gaining acceptance is that of leaving out full-stops in the case of an organisation that is better known by its initials. (See those marked \* above.)

Another group of initials acceptable without full-stops is composed of those initials that form new 'words':

NALGO, UNO (Uno), UNESCO (Unesco), UNICEF, NATO (Nato), RoSPA, Ernie, Wrens, WHO.

Other initials tend to keep the full-stops, e.g. i.e., e.g., a.m., p.m., B.A., B.Sc., etc.
N.B. A comma is required between a person's name and his title, e.g. Rev. P. C. Shuttle, M.A., B.D.

**Exercise 2**  Extend the following table to include all the initials—together with their meanings—referred to so far in this section.

| Initial | Meaning | Initial | Meaning |
|---------|---------|---------|---------|
| S.E.N. | State Enrolled Nurse | S.R.N. | State Registered Nurse |
| T.U.C. | | G.N.C. | |

With *contractions*, the last letter of the contracted form is the same as the last letter of the full word. Here much latitude is given to the writer: full-stops are not necessary, but are often preferred, particularly by examiners: e.g.

Ltd. or Ltd    Dr. or Dr    Mr. or Mr
Rd. or Rd      Sq. or Sq    St. or St (for Street or Saint).

1st, 2nd, 3rd, 4th, etc. have no full-stops. These are *symbols* and not contractions in the true sense of the word.

Generally, *abbreviations* are followed by stops, e.g. Capt., Rev., Ald., Prof., Jan., Feb., (but preferably Professor, January and February), viz.

Abbreviations such as *prefab, pub, fridge, log* (logarithm), *polio, bra*, together with their plural forms, have no full-stops. They are accepted words. On the other hand, abbreviations that have not been fully accepted into popular usage retain the full-stop, e.g. *exam., maths., lab.*

Plurals of initials are formed by adding 's', e.g. M.P.s, J.P.s, G.P.s. N.B. an M.P.'s salary, a J.P.'s understanding, a G.P.'s qualifications.

(2) Full-stops are also used to separate hours and minutes when they are given in figures, e.g. 2.15 a.m. or 02.15; 4.20 p.m. or 16.20; 9.10 p.m. or 21.10.

**Exercise 3**   (a) Express the following in continental style:

1.10 a.m.   6.20 p.m.   11.45 p.m.   10.30 a.m.   3.15 a.m.
6 a.m.      10 a.m.     noon         midnight     6.00 p.m.

(b) Re-write the following in British style:

14.30    18.30    21.00    03.15    09.00
13.30    00.30    22.10    05.20    19.50

**Exercise 4**   Study the following passages very carefully, and then re-write them inserting capital letters and full-stops where you think necessary.

(1) further extensions in life expectancy and fresh advances in the struggle against disease were predicted by u thant secretary-general of the united nations, in a message for the world health assembly, which last week celebrated who's 20th anniversary at a special session in the palais des nations. (*Nursing Mirror*, 17 May, 1968.)

(2) the nursing profession was vitally important to the country's economy ald w harrison, mp for wakefield, said on Saturday, when he presented prizes and certificates to nurses of the wakefield 'a' group schools of nursing. (*Yorkshire Post*, 20 September, 1965.)

(3) lord savile, in presenting awards to student nurses at st james's hospital, leeds, yesterday, gave his personal definition of the qualities of a nurse nursing, he said, was a vocation, and demanded kindness, self-sacrifice, and the spirit of service a nurse should enter the profession with a sense of duty, good humour, deft hands, and the willingness to obey (*Yorkshire Post*, 25 September, 1965.)

(4) the duchess of northumberland scholarship for 1968/9 was awarded to miss betty may barchard, srn, rscn, an administrative sister at hammersmith hospital, london miss doreen turnbull, srn, scm, assistant matron of newcastle general hospital, was awarded the sir james knott scholarship.

(5) the first nursing textbook to be included in a cheap series of textbooks available only to developing african and asian countries is miss w e

hector's modern nursing the english languages book society is a govern-
ment-sponsored project run in conjunction with publishers and the
british council whereby special editions of standard british textbooks are
made available at very low cost to the developing countries. (*Nursing
Times*, 29 October, 1965)

**(III) THE COMMA** indicates the shortest pause in reading or speaking. It is
the one punctuation mark that requires the application of more intuitive good
sense than mere skill in applying the rules; for although the rules are very
useful, the insertion of a comma on each occasion indicated by the rules will
result in a very confusing style indeed. One must use commas sparingly, but
not too sparingly.

Some of the main uses of the comma are set out below.

(1) **When two or more of the same part of speech follow each other,
they are generally separated by commas, e.g.**

 (a) The wallchart contained simple drawings of a probe, a scalpel, a
   clamp, a chisel, a mallet, and an osteotome. (*Nouns*)
 (b) The neglected child's teeth were rotten, chipped, and dirty. (*Adjectives*)
 (c) The surgeon carried out the operation swiftly, skilfully and con-
   fidently. (*Adverbs*)

(The comma is often omitted when the last two items are separated by the
conjunction 'and'.)

(2) **Commas are used to separate phrases or clauses occurring in
series.** In the following example, taken from Baillière's *Pocket Book of
Ward Information*, both phrases and clauses occur. (Can you pick them
out?)

 Decrease in the urinary output (oliguria) occurs in nephritis, acute
 renal failure, any condition which reduces the blood supply of the
 kidneys, circulatory failure from any cause, cardiac failure.

(3) **When words (or phrases) are IN APPOSITION, they are enclosed
in commas,** e.g. The matron, Miss J. Pointer, accompanied the doctor
on his rounds.

The above sentence appears to have two subjects, 'The matron' and 'Miss
Pointer'. As both refer to the same person, one is said to be *in apposition*
to the other. The same can apply to the object of a sentence, e.g. The nurse
accompanied the patient, Mr Crossman, to the X-Ray Department.

(4) Examine the following sentence: 'Nurse Johnson, you must endeavour to
adopt a more tactful attitude.' Again there appear to be two subjects,
'Nurse Johnson' and 'you'. In this case, though, 'Nurse Johnson' is used
to draw the attention of the nurse concerned. It is a **salutation,** and Nurse
Johnson, as the person spoken to, is the **subject of address.**

 *Commas are used to separate the subject of address from the rest of the
 sentence,* e.g.

  *Miss Johnson,* where are you going?
  Where are you going, *Miss Johnson?*
  Do you realise, *Miss Johnson,* that what you have done is a serious
  breach of discipline?

N.B.   The subject of address need not be the name of a person, e.g.

Are you aware, *young man*, what your discovery means?

(5) **Commas are often used after 'Yes' and 'No' when they open sentences, particularly in conversation,** e.g.

'No, I won't be able to come out tonight,' she said sadly into the phone.

(6) **Commas are frequently used to separate certain words and phrases from the remainder of the sentence,** e.g.

The influence of Lister's discovery of antiseptics, *however*, must not be forgotten.

Other words and phrases that come into this category include:

*therefore, nevertheless, accordingly, moreover, consequently, indeed, in fact, perhaps, for instance, finally, in the first place, etc.*

**Exercise 5**   (a) Use each of the above words and phrases in sentences to illustrate this particular use of the comma.

(b) Add to the above list at least *ten* more examples of similar words and phrases.

(7) **The comma is used before a direct quotation,** e.g.

The disgruntled young cadet said, 'It's fine for her. She's an S.R.N. and can afford to buy expensive clothes.'

N.B.   When a quotation comes from a book or a formal speech, or when a long pause is required, a colon is generally substituted for a comma: e.g.

Of the book *A Child is Born*,\* the *Nursing Times* wrote: 'This slim book of 58 pages is a photographic record of a normal delivery accompanied by a text written especially for lay people. The book is primarily for young married couples.'

\* *A Child is Born*, Dally, A. and Sweering, R., Peter Owen, 1965, £1·25.

(8) **Generally, adverbial phrases and clauses (see pp. 66–8) are followed by commas when they open sentences,** e.g.

Having removed the child's clothing, the doctor was able to see the extent of the injury.
An hour after she had given the injection, the night nurse reported that the was responding to the drug.

(9) **Pairs of commas are used to enclose words, phrases or sentences in parenthesis.** (A *parenthesis* is a word or group of words inserted into a sentence grammatically complete without it.)

As a pair of dashes or brackets may also be used to enclose a parenthesis, it is difficult to decide which to use where. There is no definite rule, but the following is a useful guide:

*For a minor parenthesis, commas will suffice; for longer ones, one has the choice between pairs of dashes or commas; to make the parenthesis really stand out, use brackets.*

e.g. (a) Sir Alexander Fleming, *known to the world as the discoverer of penicillin*, was made a Fellow of the Royal Society in 1945.

(b) Man belongs—*with lemurs, monkeys and apes*—to the group called primates.

(c) Cockroaches hide in cracks where there is some heat—*as, for instance, behind heating pipes*—and come out at night.
(It will be noticed that where the parenthesis itself contains commas, dashes are used to avoid confusion.)

(d) B.L.B. masks are manufactured in two sizes (*adult and child*) and two patterns (*nasal and oronasal*).

**Exercise 6** Study the following very carefully, and then re-write them correctly punctuated. (The extracts have been taken from John Gibson's *Human Biology*, Faber and Faber, 1960).

(1) the *femoral artery* the main artery of the leg is a continuation of the external iliac artery and enters the thigh at the middle of the groin.

(2) the liver the largest gland in the body lies in the upper right part of the abdomen just below the diaphragm being protected in the front and at the side by the lower ribs and costal cartilages.

(3) a human being is created by the fusion of a female cell the ovum with a male cell the spermatozoon the process being called fertilisation.

(4) proteins are provided mainly by meat fish eggs poultry milk cheese nuts and some vegetables; carbohydrates by sugar potatoes bread cake cereals and other grain products; fats by butter margarine cream oils fat meat and eggs.

(5) at birth a baby has to adjust rapidly to new circumstances for the first nine months of his life he has been carefully protected cushioned by fluid and muscle fed without any effort on his part provided automatically with all he has required kept in darkness and protected from most of the harmful bacteria; and now he is exposed to the difficulties and dangers of independent life.

**(IV) THE SEMI-COLON** The semi-colon is a punctuation mark used when the writer requires a stronger pause than that offered by the comma (particularly when dealing with a series of clauses), yet not as definite as a full-stop. It has four main uses:

(1) **The semi-colon is used to join two sentences that are so closely related in meaning that their separation would be artificial,** e.g.

The use of penicillin was bound to spread; it was so effective.

In the same way, sentences that are in contrast to or are explanatory of each other are joined by the semi-colon, e.g.

Blood from the head and arms is returned to the heart by the *superior vena cava; the inferior vena cava* brings the blood from the lower regions of the body.

(2) **Series of clauses (whether main or subordinate) are separated by semi-colons if commas are considered too weak,** e.g.

Smoke can be a serious threat to health. It reduces the amount of sunshine that reaches the earth; causes a deposit of carbon in the lungs and thoracic glands; and retards the growth of vegetables. (*Health, Personal and Communal*, Gibson, J. Faber and Faber, 1959.)

(3) **The semi-colon is also used to separate the main items in a list, particularly if some of the items are sub-divided,** e.g.

> (a) The first-aid box contained: a bottle of aspirin tablets, half empty; two rolls of bandage, two inches wide; a tin of antiseptic ointment; a wad of cotton-wool, some of it soiled; a tin of 'Elastoplast'; and a pair of cheap, partly-rusted scissors.

The colon after 'contained'—and after 'include' in the example below—is optional.

> (b) It was agreed that there should be an increase of one week's annual leave to operate from April 1, 1968, for certain grades of staff. The grades will include: matrons of nurseries (day and residential); supervisory matrons; all grades between the enrolled nurse and deputy matrons in nurseries; staff nursery nurses; State Registered Nurses (clinical nurses); and enrolled nurses. (*Nursing Mirror*, 24 May, 1968.)

(4) **A semi-colon may also be used with effect to replace a comma, if emphasis is needed to stress the remaining part of the sentence.** The semi-colon is also a particularly good mark to use when there is a temptation to use 'And' or 'But' to open a sentence. Instead of opening a new sentence, use a semi-colon, e.g.

> He looked forward to the operation with much optimism; but he must have known that surgery, even if successful, could not return to him the full use of his legs.

In the following sentence, we could have avoided opening the second 'sentence' with 'But' had we used a semi-colon:

> At one time the term *pyrogen* was limited to substances produced by water-borne bacteria which gave rise to fevers when injected. *But* nowadays the term can be used to cover all substances which, when injected, particularly by intravenous route, produces febrile reactions.

**(V) THE COLON** Of all the punctuation marks, the colon is one of the easiest to use. Its main uses are as follows, the one most frequently used being the first:

(1) **to introduce a list,** e.g.

> (a) The *colon* is composed of four parts: ascending, transverse, descending and pelvic.

> (b) In many conditions, specimens are required for bacteriological examination in order to identify the micro-organisms responsible. Materials required for such examination include:
>
> > throat and nose swabs,
> > swabs from wounds,
> > sputum,

stools,
urine,
blood,
pleural and ascitic fluid,
cerebro-spinal fluid.
(*Baillière's Pocket Book of Ward Information.*)

(c) Arsenic poisoning can produce many effects, some of which include: dermatitis, ulceration and pigmentation of the skin, inflammation of the eyes, throat and larynx; neuritis, especially of the legs; headache, giddiness, drowsiness and impairment of mental faculties.
(*Health, Personal and Communal*, John Gibson, Faber and Faber.)

(2) **to end a sentence, the meaning of which is to be expanded in the next,** e.g.

One of two things can happen to an ovum: it can be fertilised and a pregnancy started, or it is not fertilized and dies.

(3) **to introduce a direct quotation, particularly one from a book or a formal speech,** e.g.

Before her execution by the Germans on 12 October 1915, Nurse Edith Cavell stated: 'Patriotism is not enough. I must have no bitterness towards anyone.'

**Exercise 7**  Study the following very carefully, and then write them out correctly punctuated. Each extract contains at least one colon or semi-colon. Some punctuation marks have been inserted for you. (The first three extracts have been taken from John Gibson's *Health, Personal and Communal*, Faber and Faber (1959); the other two, from *Human Biology* (1960) by the same author.)

(1) crockery washed with a detergent should be swilled under a hot tap and stood to dry it should not be dried with a teacloth which may have become dirty or infected.
(2) unsuitable sites for building on are wet clay long-lying land likely to become waterlogged sand lying above an impervious layer and therefore likely to be wet land that has been built up by rubbish-tipping and alluvial subsoil which is ground washed down by a river or stream.
(3) a bedbug is a small insect with an oval, flat body and six legs by day it hides in cracks and crevices in walls and furniture by night it comes out to suck blood from man.
(4) Fat can be a broken down so producing energy b used in the tissues c stored in the fat depots of the body, of which the main ones are in the abdomen and under the skin or d converted into glucose.
(5) How much a joint can move is controlled by a number of factors the shape of the bones the attachment of ligaments the pull of muscles and the meeting of soft parts such as the thigh on the abdominal wall.

**(VI) THE QUESTION MARK**  Like the colon, this is one of the easiest punctuation marks to use. However, carelessness on the part of the user often leads to its misuse; and too frequently it is omitted altogether.
    It is used at the end of a *direct quotation* instead of a full-stop, not in

addition to it. (It is incorrect to write.? or ?.) It is also incorrect to use a question mark after an *indirect quotation.*

Study the following carefully:

(a) 'Have you attended to young John Smith, Nurse Philips?' enquired the doctor politely. (*Direct quotation.*)
    **but**
    The doctor asked Nurse Philips if she had attended to young John Smith. (*Indirect quotation*—so no question mark.)
(b) 'Have you read Edith Cavell's life story?' the lecturer asked.
(c) 'Do you realise the importance of these examinations,' the matron asked, 'and what success in them will bring?'

N.B. in (c) the question mark comes at the end of the two-part question.

**(VII) THE EXCLAMATION MARK**  The exclamation mark is used after interjections, and phrases and sentences expressing such emotions as joy, surprise, fear, and so forth.

e.g. Oh! Ugh! What a beautiful day! O, the poor child!

N.B. Do not use the exclamation mark excessively, as in the following advertisement:
    'Painaway' tablets kill pain! Quick!! Quicker than ever before!!!

**(VIII) THE HYPHEN**  The hyphen is a mark used for word-building; it shows that two or more words are to be considered as one compound word,

e.g. birth-rate, cross-section, half-hour, half-dozen, loud-speaker, new-comer, off-hand, pre-eminent, second-hand, son-in-law, surgeon-in-chief.

However, occasions frequently arise when the hyphen is dispensed with altogether, and the compound word becomes one single word, e.g. tonight, smallpox, tomorrow, lifelike, childbirth, lifelong, newfangled, foodstuffs, stepfather.

Then there is an ever-growing list of words that are hyphenated in some books and not in others, e.g. textbook, text-book, text book; year book and yearbook; re-open and reopen; reappear and re-appear.

In medical terminology, the use of hyphens seems most contradictory. According to the Oxford University Press, *ante-mortem* is hyphenated, *antenatal* is not; *anti-smallpox* is, *antibacterial* is not. The same applies to micro-culture, microphotograph; blood-flow, blood infection; extra-articular, extravascular; mid-ventral, midbrain, etc.

One might conclude—with some justification—that as far as hyphens are concerned, there are no hard-and-fast rules to follow. The only advice seems to be: *When in doubt, consult a dictionary.* Even so, the following 'rules' are offered as guides:

(1) When prefixes are used to form compound words of very *recent* origin, the hyphen is used, e.g. anti-bomb, pre-nursing, pro-pill, non-intervention. The hyphen is also used to avoid unsightly combinations (e.g. co-operative, re-enter, mis-spelt) or to avoid confusion (e.g. re-form, re-act, re-cover.)

When a prefix is used before a word beginning with a capital letter, a hyphen is again necessary, e.g. non-Christian, pro-American, anti-Russian.
(2) Compound cardinal and ordinal numbers require hyphens, e.g. twenty-one, twenty-first; thirty-seven, thirty-seventh; two-hundredth (but two hundred and sixty-four), three-quarters; two-thirds.
(3) The hyphen is used when two or more words are joined to form an adjective,

    e.g. hard-and-fast rules; run-of-the-mill duties; a well-known fact; a highly-skilled surgeon; a poverty-stricken neighbourhood; a cross-eyed child; a brick-red building; a four-wheeled trolley.

**Exercise 8** Examine the following very carefully, and then re-write them correctly punctuated. Pay particular attention to question marks, exclamation marks and hyphens.

(1) 'Sir, what is the address of the Anglo Danish Society,' asked the *au pair* girl.
(2) 'The very thought of it repulses me,' he roared in anger. 'You're nothing but an ungrateful wretch.'
(3) During the roman and preroman periods, the doctors of greece were preeminent in the world of medicine.
(4) 'Are you asking me if I'm antipill or antibirthcontrol,' the speaker asked the man in the audience.
(5) The Duke's reply, to the point and straight off the cuff, developed into an interesting talk on the foolishness of this antinegro attitude prevalent among a certain section of the community.

**(IX) INVERTED COMMAS**
(1) **The main use of inverted commas is to enclose direct quotations, whether** *said, written* or *thought*, e.g.

    (a) '*Among the many qualities a nurse must have,*' explained the Youth Employment Officer, '*are kindness and sympathy.*'
    (b) The book stated: '*The diseases against which inoculation is available are: smallpox, diphtheria, typhoid and paratyphoid fevers, whooping cough, poliomyelitis, tuberculosis and tetanus.*'
    (c) '*If he phones me again tonight,*' she thought, '*I'll tell him what I really think of him.*'

The words in italics, being the **exact** words said, written or thought, are known as *direct quotations*, and are enclosed in quotation marks. In *reported* (or *indirect*) *speech*, no quotation marks are used.

(2) **Inverted commas—usually single ones—are used around words that in print would appear in italics:**

    (a) *to indicate titles of books, magazines, films, radio and TV programmes,* e.g. 'Steptoe and Son', 'The World at One', 'Outline of Human Anatomy'; the 'Nursing Times' **but** 'The Times', for 'The' is part of the newspaper's title.
    (b) *around trade names,* e.g. 'I enjoy a cup of "Ovaltine" before going to bed,' she said.

(c) *in Botany, around the name of the genus and species,* e.g. 'Sambucus nigra' (Elder), 'Viscum album' (Mistletoe), 'Hyoscyamus niger' (Henbane).

(d) *around the names of groups and strains of bacteria,* e.g. 'Streptococcus viridans', 'Bacillus anthracis'.

N.B. In (c) and (d) capital letters are used for the genus and group, and lower case letters for the species and strain that follow.

(3) **Inverted commas are also used to indicate a slang word or phrase,**

e.g. 'Nurse Smith, when one of the patients dies, we do not say he has "kicked the bucket". We use far more refined expressions.'

N.B. To stress a word, underlining may be used, e.g.

'I am definitely not going to read that book,' she said indignantly.

**Exercise 9**   Re-write the following correctly punctuated.
(1) matron i refuse to attend that patient again said the young nurse rather indignantly he is ill mannered un-cooperative and utterly selfish
(2) in bacteriology stated the pamphlet one's enemies are so small that they cannot be fought face to face
(3) last week said mary he took me to  see arnold wesker's chips with everything it's  a man's play and isn't for sweet young girls like us
(4) inserting the slide into the microprojector for the second time dr mansfield turned again to his audience of nurses there ladies he said after a slight pause is a perfect example of the bacillus anthracis, the little chappie who causes anthrax
(5) hitler's master race didn't materialise the article stated because medical science was not at that time sufficiently developed today such a scheme is not only possible it is probable.

**Exercise 10**   Before attempting to punctuate the following conversation, that takes place between a young house doctor and a group of high-spirited nurses, make a note of the following:

N.B.   (a) that a new paragraph is opened when the speaker changes.
   (b) that commas, full-stops, exclamation marks and question marks come **within** the quotation marks, e.g.
   ——?' he queried.   ——!' he yelled.
   ——,' he said, laughing. ——.'
N.B.   (c) that it is a mistake—frequently made—to place a full-stop and a question mark (or exclamation mark) together,
   e.g. ——?.'   ——!.' THESE ARE INCORRECT.
N.B.   (d) that 'Yes' and 'No', when they open sentences, and *Subjects of Address* are separated from the remainder of the sentence by commas (see *Commas,* pp. 119–121).
N.B.   (e) that it is incorrect to use a capital letter to open the second part of a quoted sentence, e.g.
   'It was fortunate for her,' said the doctor, 'that we operated when we did.'

It is incorrect to write

| ——doctor. 'That—— | (Or) | ——doctor, 'That—— |

Study the following passage very carefully, and set it out correctly punctuated. Pay particular attention to paragraphing, quotation marks, capital letters and question marks. **Be warned—it is a difficult passage.**

the new house doctor a young man in his middle twenties should have realised that the four student nurses standing in a group outside matlock ward were up to something but intuition the gift of so many doctors was not one of his strong points good morning doctor said one of the girls cheerfully good morning came the courteous reply while one of the girls covered a muffled giggle the tallest of the nurses edged towards the young doctor you must be mr matthews no he replied no im not mr matthews the only matthews I know here is the chief heart specialist and hes a very eminent man but you look eminent giggled one of the girls he is also very old he paused very briefly and coughed slightly as for me he added im new in fact this is my first day new are you this time the voice came from a dark haired rather dumpy young girl with a strong west country burr in her voice in that case you must be the new surgeon whos come over from st bartholomews to take over gynaecology no im not the new surgeon from barts either my names reed walter reed and ive come to put an end to yellow jack replied the now indignant young doctor who had at last cottoned on to the antics of the nurses yellow jack queried the tall one again in an attempt to regain the initiative yellow jack whos he hes a chinaman im going to operate on this morning at that he turned away a faint smile beginning to flicker across his face as he turned into matlock ward he caught the tail end of several mixed up conversations proper little kildare isnt he just like emergency ward 10 give me dr findlays casebook anyday the sound of the double doors of the ward swinging back behind him completely shut out the sounds from the corridor here was a new world a serious one that left little time for the fun and games of the outside.

**(X) THE APOSTROPHE**   The apostrophe has two main uses.
(1) *to indicate the omission of a letter or letters from a word*
   The apostrophe is used to show *omissions* from the beginning or end of words in affected or slovenly speech, and in *contractions* such as *don't* and *isn't* in informal speech, e.g.

'If he's gone fishing, he can't be at 'ome, can he?' said Mrs Smith rather sharply.

N.B. (a)   Make sure the apostrophe is in the correct place. For instance, in *haven't* the apostrophe replaces the *o*, so it should **not** be written *have'nt* or *havent*, two common mistakes. The same applies to *isn't*, *couldn't*, *wouldn't*, *don't*, etc.
   (b)   Do not use an apostrophe in bus (omnibus), phone (telephone), plane (aeroplane).
   (c)   *it's* = *it is* or *it has*. (It is not used to show possession. Similarly the apostrophe is not used in *yours*, *ours*, *hers*, *theirs*.)

(2) *to indicate possession.* The student is asked to pay particular attention to this section, for it is here where errors are often made. Here are the rules for its use:

(a) If the noun is **singular**, then **'s** is used,

e.g. a doctor's qualifications; the nurse's left hand;
a teacher's textbook; the matron's long-service record.

(b) If the noun is plural, then **s'** is used,

e.g. the girls' hairstyles; the boys' club;
the nurses' hostel; the ladies' clothes.

(c) If the noun is **plural** but does **not** end in **s**, then the singular form (**'s**) is used, e.g.,

children's ailments; women's diseases; the workingmen's club.

Note the use of the apostrophe in the following:

one's manners; Mr Humphrey's house; I am going to my aunt's (or the butcher's, baker's, grocer's); today's weather; next month's duty rota; two weeks' time; a two hours' journey; a month's pay; three months' notice; a patient of Dr. Smith's; Dr. Smith's patient; Chain and Florey's work on penicillin.

**Exercise 11**   Re-write the following, correctly punctuated.

(1) During the eight days journey through space, the astronauts temperature remained constant.
(2) The childrens ward was situated near the hospitals rear entrance.
(3) The matrons pride in her staffs efficiency was often voiced to visitors.
(4) A timely visit to the doctors often saves trouble later.
(5) 'Its not my fault that the dogs broken its leg,' moaned the boy.

# Part VII

# SOME USEFUL AUDIO-VISUAL MATERIAL

## Abbreviations:

C      Colour
B/W    Black and white
Fs     Filmstrip
Wc    Wallchart
Pp    Purchase price
Hc    Hire charge
F      Free
Fl     Free loan
TsN    Teachers' notes
SK    Study kit

Note: All films are 16 mm

BTFL   British Transport Film Library, Melbury House, Melbury Terrace, N.W.1. Catalogue 25p.

CEWC   Council for Education in World Citizenship, 25 Charles Street, W.1.

CFC   Concord Film Council, Nacton, Ipswich, Suffolk. Catalogue 20p.

CFL   Central Film Library, Government Buildings, Bromyard Avenue, Acton, London, W3 7JB. Main catalogue 35p.

CG   Common Ground Filmstrips, Longman Group, Pinnacles, Harlow, Essex.

CT   Camera Talks, 31 North Row, London, W1R 2EN.

DW   Diana Wyllie Ltd., 3 Park Road, Baker Street, N.W.1. Free catalogue.

EB   Encyclopaedia Britannica International Ltd., Dorland House, 18–20 Regent Street, London S.W.1. Free catalogue.

EP   Educational Productions Ltd., East Ardsley, Wakefield, Yorkshire. Free catalogue.

FFL   *Foundation Film Library. (Information from Education Foundation for Visual Aids, 33 Queen Anne Street, London, W.1.)

GSV   Guild Sound & Vision (formerly Sound Services Ltd.), Kingston Road, London SW19 3NR. Library Membership £3; catalogue only £1.

JP   Jackdaw Publications, 30 Bedford Square, London, W.C.1.

PCET   Pictorial Charts Educational Trust, 132–8 Uxbridge Road, London W.13.

PFB   Petroleum Film Bureau, 4 Brook Street, Hanover Square, W1Y 2AY.

Pfizer   Pfizer Film Library, Sandwich, Kent. Free catalogue.

RFL   Rank Film Library, Rank Audio Visual Ltd., PO Box 70, Great West Road, Brentford, Middx. Catalogue 25p.

* The Educational Foundation for Visual Aids offers to teachers and others interested in visual aids a service known as 'VENISS' (Visual Education National Information Service for Schools). The annual subscription of £3·50 entitles a member to receive a set of E.F.V.A. catalogues and leaflets, the monthly magazine *Visual Education* (the July number of which acts as a yearbook) and allowances on certain books.

Another useful source of information on visual aids is the *Treasure Chest for Teachers*, published by the Schoolmaster Publishing Co. (N.U.T.) 1969, 50p.

## Places to visit

**Wellcome Historical Medical Museum and Library,** The Wellcome Building, Euston Road, London, N.W.1. Open Mon–Fri (10–5), except Bank Holidays. Admission free.

**Royal College of Surgeons' Museum,** Lincoln's Inn Fields, London, W.C.2. Admission by application to the Secretary.

**The Science Museum,** Exhibition Road, South Kensington, London, S.W.7. Open weekdays (10–6), Sundays (2.30–6). Closed Christmas Day and Good Friday. Admission free.

**Constantly rising prices make it impossible to give correct current prices for all the audio-visual material referred to below. The prices quoted are offered as a guide, for purposes of comparison only.**

## HISTORY OF MEDICINE

*A History of Medicine:* Fs; B/W; TsN; Hulton (1950); FFL; Pp £1·25.

*The History of Medicine* (two 3¾ ips tapes) Student Recordings (1971) E.F.V.A. £3·20 each.

*Great Names in Biology* (Harvey, Van Leeuwenhoek, Carolus Linnaeus, Darwin, Pasteur, Mendel): Fs; C; EB; Pp £2.

*Man Against Disease:* Fs; B/W; TsN; Hulton (1952): FFL; Pp £1.

*Florence Nightingale:* Fs; C; TsN; CG (1958); FFL; Pp £1·25.

*Florence Nightingale:* C; Wc; TsN; Post Office Postal Services, Publicity Division, Postal Headquarters Building, St Martins-le-Grand, London EC1A 1HQ. Free.

*The Lady with the Lamp:* Fs; C; TsN; EP (1952); Pp £1·90.

*The Lady with the Lamp:* 1 hr 46 mins; FFL; Hc £6·50.

*Pasteur and Microbes:* Fs; B/W; TsN; CG (1954); FFL; Pp £1·25.

*Pasteur and the Germ Theory:* SK; JP No. S3; Pp 80p.

*Harvey and the Circulation of the Blood:* SK; JP No S6; Pp 80p.

*Darwin and Evolution:* SK; JP No S4; Pp 80p.

*Lister and Antisepsis:* Fs; B/W; TsN; CG (1955); FFL; Pp £1·25.

*The Fight Against Bacteria:* C; 15 mins; TsN; FFL; Hc £1·50.

*Man's Microbe Enemies:* (Parts 1 & 2); Fs; B/W; Hulton (1952); Pp £1 ea.

*Victory over Pain:* B/W; 20 mins; FFL; Hc £1 (7 days).

*Vaccination and You:* Fs; C; TsN; DW; Pp £2·50.

*Vaccination and Immunisation:* Fs; C; TsN; DW; Pp £2·50.

*Sugar Lump Vaccines:* B/W; 20 mins; Pfizer; Fl.

*Exit Polio:* B/W; 10 mins; Pfizer; Fl.

*Birth of a Drug:* Fs; C; TsN; DW; Pp £2·50.

*Penicillin:* Fs; C; TsN; CT (1956); Pp £3·50.

*Discovery—Penicillin:* C (cartoon); 12 mins (1964); C.O.I./CFL; Hc 80p.

*The Antibiotics and Terramycin:* C; 20 mins; Pfizer; Fl.

*The Curies and Radium:* Fs; B/W; TsN; CG (1958); Pp £1·50.

*Marie Curie—Sklodowska:* B/W; 30 mins; (1967); Fl; Distributed by Films of Poland, 16 Devonshire Street, London, W.1.

*The Discovery of Radioactivity:* C; 15 mins; TsN; 1965; FFL; Hc £2 (7 days).

*Immunity:* Fs; C; TsN; CT (1966); Pp £3·50.
*Immunisation:* B/W; 10 mins; EB; FFL; Hc 75p.

## SOCIAL WELFARE AND COMMUNAL HEALTH

The official handbooks produced by local authorities are an important source of information in this field. Generally these can be purchased relatively cheaply, or obtained free of charge on request to the Clerk to the Council concerned. Consult *Whitaker's Almanack* for addresses. Also of interest are the annual Health Reports obtainable from your local M.O.H.

*Health Services in Britain:* B/W; 14 mins; 1962; CFL; Hc 90p.
*Britain's Health Service:* C; Wc; TsN; PCET; Pp 62½p.
*Rotherham Up-to-date:* C; 25 mins; Free loan on request to Town Clerk's Office, Rotherham, Yorkshire.
*The Health of the Community:* Wc; C; PCET; Pp 50p.
*The Social Services:* Fs; B/W; TsN; CT (1956); FFL; Pp £2·10.
*The Health Visitor:* Fs; C; TsN; CT (1960); FFL.
*The Home Help:* Fs; C; TsN; CT (1963); FFL; Pp £3·15.
*By Whose Hand* (Food hygiene in public places): C; 16 mins; Domestos (1962); CFL; Fl.
*The Public Health Inspector:* C; Fs; TsN; CT (1957); FFL; Pp £3·15.
*The Medical Officer of Health:* Fs; B/W; TsN; EP (1957); Pp £1·15.
*The Historical Background of Water Supply*
   Part 1: Roman Times to Seventeenth Century.
   Part 2: Eighteenth Century to Twentieth Century.
   Fs; B/W; 1951; FFL; Pp 40p each.
*Your Water Supply:* C; 22 mins; British Waterworks Association; FFL; Hc £2·25.
*Air Pollution:* Fs; B/W; TsN; CT (1954) FFL; Pp £2·10.
*Air Pollution* (parts 1 & 2): Fs; C; DW (1970); FFL; Pp £3 ea.
*Clean Air:* C; 20 mins; Shell-Mex and BP (1962); CFL; Fl.
*Guilty Chimneys:* B/W; 19 mins; Gas Council (1962); CFL; Fl.
*World Health Advances:* Photographic Display; CEWC, Fl.
*Let there be Life:* Fs; B/W; United Nations Film Board; FFL; Pp 50p.
*Malaria:* C; Wc; EP; Pp 15p.
*Malaria:* B/W; 18 mins; Shell (1959); PFB; Fl.
*The Plague and the Fire of London:* SK; JP No 2; Pp 80p.
*Shaftesbury and the Working Children:* SK; JP No 7; Pp 80p.
*Elizabeth Fry and Prison Reform:* SK; JP; Pp 80p.
*The Black Death:* SK; JP; Pp 80p.
*Drugs:* C; Wc; TsN; PCET; Pp 62½p.

## HOSPITAL ORGANIZATION: NURSING: GENERAL PRACTICE

*Twelve Nurses Look at Nursing:* B/W; 32 mins; ABC Television (1964); CFL; Hc £1·35.
*People at Work—the Almoner:* B/W; 19 mins; Associated-Redifusion (1964); CFL; Hc 90p.
*Something to Offer* (Nursing in a mental hospital): C; 22 mins; Department of Health (1969); CFL; Hc £1·60.
*Day Out, Day In* (a day in a large hospital): C; 21 mins; Department of Health (1969); CFL; Hc £1·60.

*One False Move* (Cross infection): B/W; 9 mins; Ministry of Health (1963); CFL; Hc 45p.

*Hospital Team in Action:* C; 16 mins; Ministry of Health (1960); CFL; Hc £1·60.

*Poise and Movement* (re. the nurse): B/W; 21 mins; Ministry of Health (1959); CFL; Hc 90p.

*Theatre Techniques for Nurses:* C; 23 mins; GSV; Fl.

*To Comfort Always:* B/W; 20 mins; Manchester Regional Hospital Board; GSV; Hc £1·25 per day.

*Nursing in Britain:* Photo display. C.O.I. (Regional Offices). Free loan.

*Mary Lewis—Student Nurse:* C; 20 mins; Ministry of Health (1960); CFL; Hc £1·60.

*Enrolled Nurse:* C; 19 mins; Ministry of Health (1962); CFL; Hc £1·60.

*Two Years to be a Nurse* (SEN): C; 20 mins; Ministry of Health (1967); Hc £1·60.

*Citizens All—the Nurse:* B/W; 26 mins; Southern Television (1965); CFL; Hc £1·35.

*Town Nurse,-Country Nurse:* B/W; 27 mins; Queen's Institute of District Nursing; GSV; Hc £1·50.

*Domiciliary Midwife:* Fs; C; TsN; 1962; FFl or CT; Pp £3·25.

*An Enquiry into General Practice:* B/W; 25 mins; Medical World; GSV; Fl.

*The Medicine Man* (Alan Wicker probes into the Pharmaceutical Industry); C; 28 mins; Aspro-Nicholas; GSV; Fl.

The following is a list of full-length 16 mm feature films on hire from the Rank Film Library, Rank Audio Visual Ltd., PO Box 70, Great West Road, Brentford, Middx.

*Nurse on Wheels:* 1 hr 26 mins; Hc £7·50. (Concerns a district nurse, and some of her and her patients' problems.)

*80,000 Suspects:* 1 hr 55 mins; Hc £7·50. (A smallpox epidemic in Bath is the vehicle that resolves the problems facing two doctors and their wives, one an ex-nurse who contracts smallpox while helping to fight the epidemic.)

*The Lady with the Lamp:* 1 hr 46 mins; Hc £6·50. (The title is self-explanatory.)

*Girl on Approval:* 1 hr 15 mins; Hc £6. (Deals with some of the problems that arise when a teenage girl is taken in by foster parents.)

*Life for Ruth:* 1 hr 31 mins; Hc £7·50 (The plot revolves around the problems that arise when a child dies when the father—on religious grounds—refuses permission for an essential blood transfusion.)

*Mandy:* 1 hr 53 mins; Hc £6·50. (Deals with the problems two parents face when they realise that their daughter is deaf and dumb.)

*Morgan, A Suitable Case for Treatment:* 1 hr 37 mins; Hc £8·50 (The film concerns itself with the fantasy world of Morgan Delt, an artist and lover of mankind, who ends up in an asylum, where he is able to reconcile himself with the world.)

*Carry on Doctor* (1 hr 35 mins; Hc £11·50) and *Carry on Nurse* (1 hr 20 mins; Hc £7·50) (Two films in a lighter vein, enabling students to compare the reality of their work in hospital—and its moments of light relief—with the glamour and humour presented by the film industry.)

*The Bramble Bush:* 1 hr 40 mins; Hc £7. (The story takes place in a small American town, and concerns a young doctor torn between compassion for his dying childhood friend and the Hippocratic Oath.)

# Part VIII
# LIST OF RECOMMENDED BOOKS

The following booklist is intended to supply the student—and the teacher—with a list of sources where the information asked for in the research and assignment sections can be obtained. A school or college library stocked with these suggested titles should be able to satisfy the demands made upon it when students carry out their research projects.

It will be found that some books will be in greater demand than others, and to meet this contingency it is suggested that at least three copies of those books marked with an asterisk (*) should be made available. It would also be helpful if back numbers of those titles marked with a dagger (†) were made available.

Current issues and back numbers of such publications as the *Nursing Times* and the *Nursing Mirror* will provide both the teacher and the student with a useful source of up-to-date information. The authors also recommend all those publications quoted within the main text. (See *Acknowledgements*, p. vi.)

## ENGLISH USAGE

*Fowler's Modern English Usage*, revised by Sir Ernest Gowers. Oxford University Press, 1965.
TREBLE, H. A. and VALLINS, G. H., *A.B.C. of English Usage*, Oxford University Press.
WOOD, F. T., *Current English Usage*, Macmillan, 1963.
BARON, Kathleen D., *Teach Yourself Spelling*, E.U.P., 1965.
BOWDEN, N. J. and GIBSON, J. C., *Better Spelling*, Macmillan, 1964.
JORDAN, J. (with Oliver Stonor). *The Awful Speller's Dictionary*, Wolfe, 1964.

## DICTIONARIES

*Chambers's Etymological Dictionary.*
*Chambers's Twentieth Century Dictionary.*
*\*Nuttall's Dictionary of English Synonyms and Antonyms*, Warne.
*Walker's Rhyming Dictionary*, Routledge and Kegan Paul.
*Chambers's Technical Dictionary*, 1964
*The Nurse's Dictionary*, Faber & Faber.
*Baillière's Nurses' Dictionary*, Baillière, Tindall & Cassell.
*Black's Medical Dictionary*, A. & C. Black, 1971.
*Pocket Medical Dictionary*, Livingstone, 1969.
*Medical and Nursing Dictionary and Encyclopaedia*, EVELYN PEARCE, Faber & Faber, 1966.
*Chronology of the Modern World*, WILLIAMS, N., Barrie & Rockliff, 1966.
*Who are They?*, JOHNSON, S., Wheaton, 1965.
*Chambers's Biographical Dictionary.*
*Webster's Biographical Dictionary*, Bell, 1968.

*Dictionary of Inventions and Discoveries*, Ed. E. F. CARTER, Muller, 1966.
*Newnes Dictionary of Dates and Anniversaries*, compiled by ROBERT COLLISON, Newnes, 1962.

## ENCYCLOPAEDIAS and GENERAL REFERENCE

†*Britain: An Official Handbook* (Annual), H.M.S.O.
*†*Whitaker's Almanack* (Annual)
*†*Daily Mail Yearbook*
**Pears Cyclopaedia* (Annual), Pelham Books, Ltd.
*Dunlop Book of Facts*, Dreghorn Publications.
*The Penguin Encyclopaedia*, Penguin Books, 1965.
*Oxford Junior Encyclopaedia* (Vol 5. *Great Lives;* Vol 10. *Law and Order;* Vol 11. *The Home*). Oxford University Press.
*The Nurse's Encyclopaedia and Guide*, Faber & Faber, 1957.
*Pocket Book of Ward Information*, Baillière, Tindall and Cassell, 1965.

## HISTORY OF MEDICINE

### (a) General

BANKOFF, G., *Milestones in Medicine*, Museum Press, 1957.
CALDER, R., *Medicine and Man*, Allen & Unwin, 1958.
CHICK, H., *et al, War on Disease, A History of the Lister Institute*, Andre Deutsch, 1971.
DAVENPORT, W. H., *The Good Physicians: A Treasury of Medicine*, Macmillan.
EDWARDES, David, *Introduction to Anatomy in 1532*. (Fascimile reproductions with English translations.)
ELWELL, F. R. and RICHARDSON, J. M., *Science and the Doctor*, Bell, 1957.
FLYNN, M. W., *Public Health Reform in Britain*, Macmillan, 1967.
GUTHRIE, D., *A History of Medicine*, Nelson, 1958.
HOWAT, A and G., *The Story of Health*, Pergamon, 1967.
INGLIS, B., *A History of Medicine*, Weidenfeld and Nicolson, 1965.
LAPAGE, G., *Man Against Disease*, Abelard-Schuman, 1964.
MAPLE, E., *Magic, Medicine and Quackery*, Robert Hale, 1968.
PIKE, E. Royston, *Human Documents of the Industrial Revolution in Britain*, Allen & Unwin, 1967.
POYNTER, F. N. L. and KEELE, K. D., *A Short History of Medicine*, Mills & Boon, 1961.
SIGERIST, Henry E., *A History of Medicine*
    Vol I : *Primitive and Archaic Medicine* (1951)
    Vol II : *Early Greek, Hindu and Persian Medicine* (1961), Oxford University Press.
SINGER, C. and UNDERWOOD, E. A., *A Short History of Medicine*, Oxford University Press, 1962.
SYLVESTER, D. W., *The Story of Medicine*, Edward Arnold, 1965.
TAYLOR, B., *Medicine*, Ward Lock Educational, 1962.
THOMPSON, W. A. R., *The Searching Mind in Medicine*, Museum Press, 1960.
TURNER, D. M., *The Book of Scientific Discovery*, Harrap, 1960.
WRIGHT, H. and RAPPORT, S., *The Amazing World of Medicine*, Gollancz, 1962.

## (b) Specific

ABEL-SMITH, B., *History of the Nursing Profession*, Heinemann, 1960.
BALDREY, P. E., *The Battle Against Bacteria*, Cambridge University Press, 1965.
BANKOFF, G., *The Story of Plastic Surgery*, Faber & Faber, 1952.
BROCKINGTON, Fraser, *A Short History of Public Health*, J. & A. Churchill, 1966
BETT, W. R., *A Short History of the Nursing Profession*, Faber & Faber, 1960.
CALDER, J. M., *The Story of Nursing*, Methuen, 1970.
COWAN, K., *Implant and Transplant Surgery*, John Murray, 1971.
DAINTON, C., *The Story of England's Hospitals*, Museum Press, 1961.
GIBSON, John, *The Development of Surgery*, Macmillan, 1968.
GRAVES, C., *The Story of St. Thomas's*, 1948.
LONGMATE, N., *Alive and Well: Medicine and Public Health, 1830 to the Present Day*, Penguin, 1972.
MARTIN, I., *From Workhouse to Welfare: The Development of the Welfare State*, Penguin, 1972.
TURNER, E. S., *Roads to Ruin: The Shocking History of Social Reform*, Penguin.

## BIOGRAPHIES

### (a) General

*Chambers's Biographical Dictionary*, 1968.
*Chambers's Dictionary of Scientists*, 1956.
*Webster's Biographical Dictionary*, G. Bell, 1963.
BANKOFF, G., *Milestones in Medicine*, 1957.
BATH, P. E., *Great Names in Medicine*, Wheaton, 1960.
CROWTHER, J. G., *Six Great Doctors*, Hamish Hamilton, 1957.
HUME, R. F., *All About Great Men of Medicine*, W. H. Allen, 1962.
JOHNSON, S., *Who are They?*, Wheaton, 1965.
KRUIF, P. de., *Microbe Hunters*, Jonathan Cape, 1963.
WILKINS, F., *Six Great Nurses*, Hamish Hamilton, 1962.
WILLIAMS, G., *Virus Hunters*, Hutchinson, 1960.
WILLIAMS, H., *Great Biologists*, Bell, 1961.
WILLIAMS, Trevor, *Biographical Dictionary of Scientists*, Black, 1969.

### (b) Individual

BIGLAND, E., *Sister Kenny*, Muller, 1960.
BURTON, M. J., *Louis Pasteur: Founder of Microbiology*, Chatto, 1964.
DOORLY, E., *Radium Woman: Life of Madame Curie*, Heinemann, 1939.
ELLIS, A. W. and WILLIS, E. C., *Laughing Gas and Safety Lamp: The Story of Humphrey Davy*, Methuen, 1951.
HARRISON *et al*, *Dr. William Harvey*, Collier-Macmillan, 1967.
KENDALL, J., *Humphrey Davy*, Faber & Faber, 1954.
MANTON, Jo, *Albert Schweitzer*, Methuen, 1955.
KEYNES, Sir Geoffrey, *Life of William Harvey*, O.U.P., 1966.
MARCUS, R. R., *William Harvey*, Chatto & Windus, 1965.
MAUROIS, A., *The Life of Sir Alexander Fleming*, Jonathan Cape, 1959, Penguin, 1963.

MAUROIS, A., *Fleming, The Man Who Cured Millions*, Methuen, 1961.
McKNOWN, R., *Marie Curie*, A. & C. Black, 1961; *She Lived for Science* (Irène Joliot-Curie), Macmillan, 1962; *Fabulous Isotopes*, Macmillan, 1964.
NICOLLE, J., *Louis Pasteur*, Hutchinson, 1961.
PAIN, N., *Louis Pasteur*, A. & C. Black, 1965.
PIKE, R. E., *Charles Darwin*, Muller, 1962.
RUBIN, E., *The Curies and Radium*, Chatto and Windus, 1962.
THOMAS, H., *Sister Kenny*, A. & C. Black, 1958.
TIBBLE, J. W. and A., *Helen Keller*, A. & C. Black, 1962.

## SOCIAL SERVICES

*Advising the Citizen* (1961), *The Story of the Citizen's Advice Bureaux* (1964) National Council for Social Service.
*The Consumer's Guide to the National Health Service*, Penguin, 1970.
*Future Structure of the National Health Service*, H.M.S.O., 1970.
*Guide to the Social Services*, Family Welfare Association, 1970.
*Health Services in Britain*, H.M.S.O., 1968.
*Public Social Services*, N.C.S.S., 1966, with 1971 supplement.
*Social Services in Britain*, H.M.S.O., 1969.
*Trends in Social Welfare*, Ed. W. A. J. Farndale, Pergamon, 1964.
*Some Books on the Social Services*, N.C.S.S., 1969.
*Voluntary Social Services: Handbook of Information and Directory of Organisations*, N.C.S.S., 1970.
BRENNAN, W. K., *Social Services*, E. J. Arnold, 1966.
CROSSMAN, RICHARD H. S., *Paying for the Social Services*, Fabian Society, 1969.
HALL, P. M., *Social Services of England and Wales*, Routledge, 1969.
HOUGHTON, D., *Paying for the Social Services*, Institute of Economic Affairs, 1969.
JOHNS, E. A., *The Social Structure of Modern Britain*, Pergamon, 1966.
MARSH, D. C., *The Welfare State*, Longman, 1970.
STROUD, J., *An Introduction to the Child Care Service*, Longman, 1965.
SWINSON, A., *A History of Public Health*, Wheaton, 1965.
*THOMAS, G. (with Dr. Ian D. Hudson), *The National Health Service and You*, Panther, 1965.
WILCOCKS, C., *Medical Advance, Public Health and Social Evolution*, Pergamon, 1966.
WILLIAMS, G., *The Coming of the Welfare State*, Allen & Unwin, 1967.

## RELATED TOPICS

BAILLIE, T. W., *From Boston to Dumfries: First Surgical Use of Ether in the Old World*, Dinwiddie (1966).
CARLISLE and CARLISLE, *Marvels of Medical Engineering*, Oak Tree Press, 1966.
CLARK-KENNEDY, A. E., *Patients as People*, Faber & Faber, 1957; *Medical Misfortunes of the Slocombe Family*, Faber & Faber, 1967.
FULLER, J., *The Day of St. Antony's Fire*, Hutchinson, 1968.
GLEMSTER, B., *The Long Safari*, Bodley Head, 1970.
IMLAH, N., *Drugs in Modern Society*, Geoffrey Chapman, 1970.

LAURIE, P., *Drugs: Medical, Psychological and Social Facts*, Penguin. (1969).
LONGMATE, N., *King Cholera*, Hamish Hamilton, 1966.
McLAUGHLIN, T., *Coprophilia or a Peck of Dirt* (Public Health and Hygiene exposed!), Cassell, 1971.
MORTON, R. S., *Veneral Diseases*, Penguin, 1970.
POYNTER, F. N. L. (Ed), *Medicine and Culture*, Wellcome Institute of History, 1969.
PITT, P., *Surgeon in Nepal*, John Murray, 1970.
SCHOFIELD, M., *The Strange Case of Pot*, Penguin, 1971.
SWINSON, A., *A Casebook of Medical Detection*, P. Davies, 1965.
WYKES, A., *The Doctor and His Enemy*, Michael Joseph, 1965.
ZIEGLER, P., *The Black Death*, Collins (1969), Penguin (1970).